THE FURTHEST DISTANCE BETWEEN TWO PINTS

FROM DRUGS & DESTRUCTION TO SOBRIETY AND SUCCESS

DEDICATION

To my two biggest fans
and my two biggest supporters:

Mom, for always cheering me on.
Amy, for always letting me be me.

To everyone who reads this book:

May you find something in these pages that inspires you, gives you
hope, encourages you, and gives you direction for your future.

CONTENTS

FOREWORD

Josh was different from the moment he answered the phone. I hadn't talked to him in five years. In fact, it took his mother, Debbi, several attempts to get me to reconnect with Josh. Against my better judgment, I picked up the phone and dialed his number.

I've known Josh since we were 12. He became part of the trio with our friend Sean and me. He was a funny kid. What I remember most about him was that he was really nice. The three of us did what young boys do. We toilet-papered houses, shot BB guns at each other, and had good, innocent fun.

I went to college, and Josh started working. When he was 19, I saw him again, but I didn't recognize him. It wasn't because time had passed. As kids, he was never the centerpoint of the story. This new Josh commanded all the attention. Josh made sure we knew all about his accomplishments, including his success at his current job-making $65,000 a year at age 19. His kindness had turned into arrogance.

Josh is a very intelligent man, but he managed to turn anything good he had going for him into destruction. The older he got, the bolder he got. The bigger his ideas and his lies, the more we grew apart. On two different occasions, I offered Josh a place to stay with me and my family, thinking that all he needed was a couple months' savings and a restart. Boy, was I wrong. He would take the time and money and further compound his issues. One of Josh's superpowers was the ability to get another chance. Even with pending embezzlement charges, Josh would land another high-paying management job. I've never seen someone do less with more. His gift was so often his curse.

I had no problem having Josh around my wife and kids because, despite his addictions, he would never harm anyone. That was part of the frustration. Josh is smart, funny, and even more so, he's a kind man. So, although he made terrible choices, he was harmless. By terrible choices, I mean everything from embezzlement and gambling to drug and alcohol addictions. These choices made it so hard to be his friend. Watching him throw away good job after good job and good person after good person got exhausting. The only thing more exhausting was listening to him rationalize or lie about both.

Even though I have a psychology degree and was a probation officer, Josh was lying to me like all my other cases and it took me longer to figure out his lies because he went out of his way to complicate the backstory of where he went wrong. I knew Josh would drink beer with a Jagermeister shot, but I never knew he had a cocaine habit until I tried to help him manage his money. He would never tell you why he was going to jail or the reason for his warrants. No one ever knew what was going on until things got worse, and then you would find out more.

My reluctance to reconnect with him was because I tried to help him several times, and each time, I realized how worse off he was.

The last straw was when he was arrested while living with me and my family in Kansas City. He was running from the law and disappeared after a few months, with some scheme to roll sushi on Grand Lake. I realized he hadn't changed. He had excuses for everything and never owned up to any of his issues. That was the last time I dealt with him. I couldn't go through it again.

Years later, you can imagine my surprise when I picked up the phone and heard someone honestly acknowledge his mistakes for the first time in twenty years. He said he was a four-time felon and had just gotten out of jail after being there for a year. That right there would have been enough of a change for me to reconnect with Josh, but on top of that, something was missing in him—in a good way. He was missing his usual grandiose plan to get rich. He finally sounded like someone who was determined to live in the real world and trying to improve himself daily. Instead of arrogance, he had humility and reasonability. This Josh was still my friend Josh, but there was something different about him. I watched Josh throw years of his life away and make empty promises that he was a changed man. For the first time in years, I believed this man on the other end of the phone was truly a changed man.

This book is the story of a man who turned his life around and finally chose to use his superpowers for good. It has been an incredible 30-year journey. I am so honored to have known Josh through it all and privileged to call him my friend.

-Chris Claybon-

INTRODUCTION

How do you take a guy who stole from every business he worked for, got high all day, drank until he passed out, and woke up to a different woman every morning and turn him into a man who is faithful to the same woman for twelve years, sober for ten years, ridiculously honest to a point where it is probably annoying, and surrounds himself with people who challenge him to be better every single day?

The answer is in the power of my story.

I want you to understand that no matter where you are in life and no matter how bad you think your life is, you are not too far gone. For four days, I woke up behind a Conex container at a hotel under construction because no one would answer the phone. I had gotten to a point in my life where people were tired of me lying to and stealing from them. I was a horrible person.

The transformation that occurred in my life was that I went from having zero relationships and only caring if I had money, sex, drugs, or alcohol to having a desire to pour into others. I realized if I am not willing to tell my story as raw and as real as it is, then what am I really doing? The glory of the story is truly who I was versus who I AM today. I was the guy with absolutely no hope whatsoever and in a state of utter despair. I saw no way out of the mess I had made of my life. I was a thief. I AM a business owner and mentor. I was an addict who lived in a dope house. I AM sober, healthy, safe, and contributing to society. I was lost and hopeless. I AM set free and hopeful. I was fatherless. I AM a child of God.

Why do you want to read this book?

My desire for those of you living the way I used to is that you will read this book and realize there is hope. I never realized that I could have this much fun while staying sober. I never realized I could have so much joy with one woman. I never realized that life could be this rewarding. I get to share it with an amazing person, live a sober life, and surround myself with sober people. I didn't think life like this was possible.

I've lived on the other side, and now I'm choosing to live this way. If this way wasn't so fun and so rewarding and so deep and so passionate and so amazing, then I would go snort a bunch of cocaine and sleep with a bunch of women and gamble a bunch of money. I'm in a position where I could be high for a long time. I have more money than I need. I'm in a position where I could manipulate a ton of people because I've gained a lot of respect and credibility and built my integrity. I'm in a position of influence and power over a lot of people's lives that I didn't have in the past. I only had it because of my words, not because I was an actual leader or because of my actions. I had it simply because I would dominate people through a conversation.

The evidence of why life is better as a sober, healthy human being is the life I now willingly choose to live every single day. I get up early and walk out my life. I go to bed early and love one woman. I choose not to lie and do my darndest not let any unwholesome talk come out of my mouth. I take every negative thought captive and make them positive, and I serve others above myself. The life I choose to live is evidence of why you should make this transformation. If it wasn't rewarding, if it wasn't fulfilling, if it wasn't amazing, if it wasn't awesome and phenomenal and fantastic and every adjective you could possibly think of, I wouldn't do it. I wouldn't do it at all.

It's higher than any drug high.

I get to do things every single day that I never dreamed were possible. I sat with a gentleman who is a professor at a business school. He has a doctorate. I graduated high school. He invited me to come speak to his students about business. I told him, "I'm a four-time felon, a drug addict, and a recovered alcoholic." He replied, "You said you were writing a book." I said, "Yes, it'll be done soon." "What's the title?" he asked. I said, "The Furthest Distance Between Two Points: From Drugs and Destruction to Sobriety and Success." He responded, "So you were that far down, huh?" I said, "Yep." He looked at me and said, "Well, I'm honored to meet you."

I challenge you to look at the facts of my life and then decide for yourself if you think there is more. At the time of the publishing of this book, I own several companies, four of which are multimillion-dollar businesses. We currently employ over 50 people, including a number of them with similar paths as mine, who now have opportunities to create new futures for themselves. Whether one-on-one or with a group of people, I get to inspire, motivate, and direct people to grow, develop, and improve their lives through the position and influence God has given me. I coach small business owners to help them grow their businesses. Last year, our average client experienced over 100% growth. I get to lead a team of exceptional people as we share the same vision and pursue the same journey to grow what God has entrusted me to build. I have a phenomenal relationship with my brothers and their children, and I live with the hope that I will have a healthy and happy relationship with my own kids. I wake up every morning next to my wife, who I love more and more every day. Our love is deeper than I could have ever imagined. My wife is my best friend, and I get to spend the rest of my life with her.

I get it. Making the change must be worth it. I knew there had to be something better in life. The life I lived had one of two endings: me dying or me in prison for a long time. Sitting in jail in Duncan, Oklahoma, I realized that I wasn't going to be able to talk my way out of what I had done. I risked a bunch of people's lives running from the cops at 130 miles per hour. I was not going to walk away from this one. That's when I reasoned that there must be something different—there had to be something better. So, I decided that day I would go try something else and see what happens.

Maybe you are in jail, just woke up from being drunk or high all night, are lying next to a woman you don't even know, or struggling with some hidden secret. Or maybe you sit in a church pew every Sunday, contemplating your life as the pastor preaches his messages as though they are directed at you. Or perhaps you are like I once was—exhausted with the life you are currently living. Have you had the thought that there has to be something better than this? Are you ready for a new path in life that will not harm you but give you hope and a future? If you are ready to change the course of your life, and you believe there's more for you, keep reading. Give me a chance to show you what happened when I asked myself these same questions.

PART 1
PROLOGUE

I was 19 years old when I followed a buddy of mine into the bathroom stall of a brewery in Oklahoma City. We were in town for his sister's wedding and had been drinking all day. It was getting late, so I told him I was going to head back to the hotel to go to sleep. I'd had enough. I was exhausted. But he said, "Come on, man. Come with me to the bathroom."

So, I did.

He put two lines of cocaine on the back of the toilet, handed me a dollar bill, and showed me how to do it. You just close one nostril and suck it all up the other one, and then you do the other side. The euphoria that I felt—the absolute transformation in my mind, body, and soul—was something that can only be understood by other addicts. I can't explain it. But at that moment, I was completely sober. I wasn't tired anymore. I was super focused.
That single moment in 1997 altered the next 18 years of my life. But my yes to cocaine started years before that day in the brewery in Oklahoma City.

PART 1

FROM DRUGS AND DESTRUCTION

1

ABANDONED AND FATHERLESS

I don't remember when my dad left. I was three. When I was five, he picked me and my two brothers up and took us somewhere a few days before my birthday. I don't even remember where or what we did. I just remember I wasn't happy. I also remember he didn't get me anything for my birthday.

I didn't speak to my dad again until I was 10. He remarried and moved to Dallas. His new wife had two kids, a daughter and a son. The son was a football coach a few miles from where we lived, so he offered to take me and my brothers to go visit my dad for Christmas. My stepbrother picked us up and drove us to Dallas. My dad had a nice house, a new Camaro, and a work truck. His wife drove a Cadillac.

We lived in HUD government apartments on food stamps.

We went home and told my mom, and she filed for child support. Before then, Dad never paid a dime. He got upset and told us that he didn't want to talk to us anymore. He accused us of betraying him and told us we were no longer his kids.

My mom desperately wanted her boys to have confidence and high character and to understand that nobody was better than us.

The Furthest Distance Between Two Points

She always made sure that we had a clean and organized home. But ultimately, we still got dropped off and picked up at Mingo Manor, in our HUD apartment, which was constantly infested with roaches from dirty neighboring apartments. We still went to buy candy with food stamps, and we still had hand-me-down and donated clothes or the cheap stuff off the Walmart racks. Even at a young age, when I got a job and earned money, I always felt less than everyone else. I bought clothes and shoes to fit in with my classmates, but I still felt like I didn't belong. I was always less than.

My mom went to school and worked all the time. I don't remember her ever sleeping. She graduated with an Occupational Therapy Degree and earned enough money for us to be able to leave the HUD apartments. She bought us a home on a corner lot over by a little elementary school. She was always there to take us to the hospital when we broke bones or put a band-aid on our scrapes and bruises. She was always present. She worked hard to give us a good life and taught my two brothers and me how to work hard. But it was hard for my mom to say I love you. When you're growing up, all you want is your mom's approval. You desperately seek for someone to tell you they're proud of you, they love you, and you are doing a good job.

So, I never understood love.

I had a lot of feelings of unworthiness. Regardless of how hard I tried or what I did, it just wasn't enough. I tried to overcompensate with everything I did because if I could paint a picture of greatness and excellence, where I came from didn't matter. But I still never felt like I fit in anywhere. I wasn't good enough because if I was who I was supposed to be and if I was a good kid, why would my dad leave? If I was worth it, why didn't he stay? If I'm not worthy enough for my dad to stay around, why would anybody think I'm worthy enough? My own father left. What does that say about me?

When I was 10, my mom enrolled me in a program called "Big Brothers Big Sisters of Oklahoma." My big brother and I developed a relationship. One day, he was supposed to pick me up and take me to the zoo. I sat outside all day long. My mom kept telling me to go play. I insisted he would show up; there's no way he won't show up; he'll be there. I kept telling my mom we were going to go to the zoo. He never came. I don't know if he had a valid reason for not coming. Maybe he had car problems or a flat tire. Thirty-five years later, I still have no clue why he didn't come. All I could think was, "Why does this keep happening to me? Who am I that this keeps happening?"

Because of the enviroment that surrounded me growing up, I thought this was all my life would ever become. I didn't have my dad to go to games like all the other kids. We didn't have money. My childhood was just me and my brothers making up games. I have lots of good memories of me and my two brothers, Jay and Jonas, playing on the playground. I had a ton of fun with my brothers, making up silly competitions. My relationship with Jay is what created my ridiculous competitiveness. Two of the greatest loves of my life, basketball and pool, came from my older brother, Jay. I wanted to be like him. I excelled in both sports because I wanted his approval. I wanted to impress him. I wanted him to be proud of me, so I put everything into his sports because he was my father figure. He took the place of my father.

One day, I was walking to the neighborhood park to play football with my brothers. When we got there, we found a guy shooting baskets. Jay was already playing basketball, but I didn't know much about the game. The man shooting hoops was Dave Terrell. He lived in the neighborhood right behind our apartments. I asked Dave if he would teach me how to play basketball. He agreed to help me.

He was a tough man. He taught me how to play basketball like Larry Bird, with the same grit, toughness, and passion. I went to the courts after school, and Dave would teach me how to shoot free throws, dribble, pass the ball, and play defense. He also taught me about being a man. As we played, Dave guided and directed me about life. He would take me to the bad parts of town to play basketball because he believed that's where toughness was created. Dave would make me shoot ten consecutive free throws before I could leave. Sometimes, I would be there for hours. That's where I learned discipline.

Even though we were in rough areas, the guys living there were kind to me and Dave. They would tell us, "It's time for you guys to leave," whenever fights would break out or gang members were approaching.

As time continued, Dave invited me on family vacations. I remember going to the Terrell Watermelon Festival multiple summers. He took me rafting, and we went floating down the river. He treated me like a family member. He showed me what was right and how to act right. Basketball became my favorite sport until I learned how to play pool.

When Jay started shooting pool at the pool hall, I decided I would learn how. A little before age 11, I walked into the pool hall be-hind our apartment complex and asked a man named Steve Wells if I could play pool. He said, "You got any money?" I said, "No, sir, I don't have any money at all." He said, "Well, if you clean the windows, sweep the floor, and clean off all the tables, I'll let you play pool." So, I did. I cleaned and then shot pool all day. Steve taught me the fundamentals of the game and how to move the cue ball around the table, make shots, and understand the physics and geometry of the game. He taught me about life.

So did the pool hall.

People were smoking, drinking, doing drugs, and in unhealthy relationships. They were also gambling, which became a way for me to make money. I figured out how to use money for my benefit. I didn't have much money, so I played a couple of weekend tournaments with a $5 buy-in and won. They were fun recreational tournaments, but the success kept me gambling. It became so easy. I wasn't nervous. I wasn't scared. It was something I was good at, and it gave me self-esteem. I found my self-worth in shooting pool because I was somebody in the pool hall. Eventually, I started gambling for larger dollar amounts. I challenged a grown man and beat him. I beat him badly. I won a $125 shooting pool when I was 11 years old. As a young kid, I used money for my benefit because that's how I saw it. That's what money was for—for me to be able to do what I wanted to do with it.

While Steve positively influenced my life, the pool hall exposed me to a lifestyle to which I would eventually succumb. At such a young age, I was surrounded by destructive relationships, sex conversations, locker room talk with guys, and the objectification of women. Everyone was a hustler. Lying for a living was normal. The goal in pool is to convince the opponent that you can't beat them, even though you can. Drugs were the norm and expected.

This time in my life was pivotal. I was 11 years old, and spending a lot of time in a pool hall, while at the same time, going to church. I attended church three to four days a week, studied the Bible every day, and talked to everybody about Jesus. Despite getting ridiculed by classmates, I even wore t-shirts that talked about Jesus on them. I still continued spending time at the pool hall.

 Even though I went to church, I didn't consider gambling wrong. Gambling was just me being better than everyone else at something, and the exchange of money was a result of my success. I continued to play pool in the pool hall and earn money for the wrong reasons. I spent money on the wrong things, including expensive shirts, shoes, and jeans, and I perverted money by gambling. I never understood the value of money. The pool hall conflicted with what I was learning in church. There was a battle going on inside me. I lived in both worlds. Eventually, the environment eroded away at my values and morals and what I should have been doing. Life in the pool hall won. It was much sexier. And I thought what I was doing was okay because all the adults around me were doing it too.

I was too young to recognize that my life was slowly eroding away, partially because I continued to have positive men enter my life. One of those men I met the summer before my twelfth birthday. My buddy and I would walk a mile and a half from our house to Hicks Park to play basketball. We always passed a little barbecue place called Back Home Barbecue. I told my friend I was thirsty and was going to go in to get a drink. That's when I met Johnny McGrew. I asked Johnny for a cup of water. He said, "Nope, nothing's free." He continued. "I'll give you an app, though," and I said, "Excuse me?" He said, "I'll give you an app. We're hiring." And he handed me a job application." A little taken aback, I said, "Oh, okay. An application. Sure, give me a job."

Johnny handed me an application, and I sat down at the table I became super familiar with over the next four years of my life. As I filled out that application, I didn't know what to put on it, so I wrote down my mom's name, address, and phone number. He said, "Is this your phone number? This is your mom?" I said, "Yes, sir." He called mom and asked if I could get my clothes dirty. My mom said yes. At age 12, I had a full-time job. I cleaned the barbecue pit that day, and he asked me to come back the next day. I worked the whole summer, making between $100 to $150 a week.

Over the next four years, I worked for Johnny. He treated me like one of his sons. He taught me about hard work and being true to my word and commitment. I worked every day that I could. I learned how to wash and scrub bathrooms, floors, dishes, and barbecue pits and how to cook and make great barbeque. I also learned how to talk to people, how to deal with customers, how to handle complaints, and how to make a customer happy.

Johnny poured time and effort into my life among all the racial divisions in the world. Why was this so significant?

Because Johnny was a black man.

He was a black man who grew up in a bad part of town in North Tulsa, made it out of the rough area, and built something for his life. He took in this little white kid and was committed to helping me grow as a person and learn how to be a man.

A Crumbling Foundation

The older I got the more uncool it became to be a Christian. That's not what the "in" crowd was doing. They were out drinking, smoking, doing drugs, and having sex. The foundation of my life wasn't as strong as I thought. The freedom to do what I wanted was more fun than following Jesus. I started talking to girls. Girls didn't want to talk about Jesus. I stopped wearing the t-shirts. They were stupid. I stopped going to church.

When I was 16, I got my first girlfriend. We fell in love. We were going to get married, have kids, and live a happy life. I knew she was going to be my wife, so one evening, I lost my virginity to her. I remember feeling horrible about it in the moment. "Oh my gosh, what have I done? I'm supposed to wait until I get married. I'm supposed to do the right thing, and that's supposed to be for my wife." But then I thought, "No way. We're going to get married, and I love her. This is going to be fantastic."

As time went on, we had problems. She cheated on me with one of my best friends and broke off the relationship. I thought my whole world was going to end. Not only was I devastated, but I compromised my morals and beliefs and lost my virginity to someone who wasn't my future wife.

I started attending church again, and then I got another girlfriend. Shortly after we started dating, we slept together. I graduated high school, and she was still in school, so I stuck around. Two weeks after I graduated high school, a buddy of mine got married, and his bachelor party was the first time I ever drank. I passed out from drinking too much. I was sick for two days. It was terrible. And then drinking became normal. I wasn't sure what I wanted to do with life, so I spent most of my time working, shooting pool, drinking, and smoking. My girlfriend went to college, which stretched our already rocky relationship. I visited her a couple times, and then she wound up fooling around with one of my best friends, so the relationship ended. Once again, I asked myself, "Why would this happen to me?" My dad left, and now the first two girls I slept with both ended up fooling around with different best friends.

One day, my buddy and I met a couple girls from out of town. We went to a local park and decided to skinny-dip in the pool. One of the neighbors called the cops. The police officer showed up and asked all of us for our identification. He told the other three to leave and then had me turn around and put my hands behind my back.

I questioned him. "Sir, what's going on? I don't understand." He told me I had a seatbelt ticket from the year before that I never paid. I had a traffic warrant out for my arrest. He told me he would take me to Tulsa County Jail, and I could bond out or pay the fine, and then they would let me go.

So that's exactly what happened. I went to jail, and the officer processed me. I was 18 years old when I went to jail for the first time. A few hours later, a buddy of mine showed up and paid the bail. Little did I know that time in jail would be the first of over thirty jail sentences throughout the next twenty years.

No Turning Back

At that time, I was living in an apartment and dating another woman. We thought we were going to get married, so we both agreed it was okay for us to have sex. We broke up, and I continued to go to the pool hall every day, pick up women, and socially drink. I was making a good living working at a restaurant and spent a lot of time with my new best friend who I met at work. We did everything together except smoke weed. I never smoked with him. One day, he invited me to his sister's wedding in Oklahoma City. That's when he put the two lines of cocaine on the back of the toilet, and I did drugs for the first time.

When we got back from Oklahoma City, I didn't do drugs again, but I knew I liked it and the lifestyle attached to it, so I knew I had to do something else. My life had zero direction. I needed to change the trajectory of my life. After a discussion with my grandfather, I decided to join the military.

2

A FATHER AND AN ABANDONER

In the fall of 1998, I enlisted in the Air Force. On December 23, 1998, the base commander decided to allow for early graduation on Christmas Eve. The training instructors told us to book a plane ticket to anywhere we wanted to go. I went to Washington, D.C., to visit my oldest brother. He was stationed there as a federal prison guard in Virginia. I flew to Virginia and spent six days inside playing cards and hanging out with my brother during a blizzard. I decided to go back to Lackland Air Force Base early because of the snowstorm. We were supposed to report back on January 5th, but I flew back on December 29th. The base was empty because most people were on leave. That is when I met a young lady. We agreed to go out on New Year's Eve. We had dinner. Neither of us was twenty-one. We didn't drink. We hung out and kissed at midnight.

I honestly don't know whose idea it was, but we decided to get a hotel room. That night, we slept together.

We hung out a couple times after that, but nothing happened. Then a few months later, she came to me and told me she was late. One of the dumbest comments I have ever made in my life was, "Late for what?"

The Furthest Distance Between Two Points

She was pregnant.

Because of how physically active her current career field in Security Forces was, the Air Force gave her the option to choose a different career field. They would not let her go through training as a pregnant woman because she might lose the baby. She just turned 18 years old, and she was pregnant.

She took a secretary job and left for training in Biloxi, Mississippi. My brother lived in Las Vegas, Nevada, and just had my oldest nephew, so I decided to go to Vegas. Before deciding to leave, my grandfather sat me down and told me not to go. He told me to go to London, Florida, Hawaii, Spain, or anywhere in Europe to get exposure to something different. There are Air Force bases all over the world. Spain would have been a good option. I spoke Spanish. Because of my career field, I could go anywhere I wanted. He told me if I go to Vegas, it will ruin the rest of my life. I didn't listen. I knew what I was doing—or so I thought. So, I chose to go to Vegas.

My grandfather was right. I loved the lights, the strip club, and the drinking, and I thrived on the lack of sleep. Even though I previously tried cocaine, I didn't do drugs in the military, but I drank a lot. I drank until I passed out somewhere. I gambled and chased women. Vegas was a vacation spot for girls. I was with somebody new every week.

The young lady, now pregnant with my child, agreed to get married so we could be stationed together. In the summer of 1999, we drove to Irvine, California, and got married in a courthouse. We sent the marriage certificate over to her first sergeant. They changed her orders, and she moved to Nellis Air Force Base in Las Vegas, Nevada.

A few months later, on October 19, 1999, my son was born.

I was 21 years old, married, and had a child. My wife was 18 years old, married to someone who didn't want to be married, and had a child that she took care of while I continued to go to work, go to the casinos, run around with other women, and leave her at the apartment. I wasn't faithful. I didn't treat her the way I should have. I wasn't a good husband. We got evicted from our off-base apartment because I didn't pay rent. I gambled the money instead. My wife called her first sergeant and asked the military to move her into base housing. She told me she wasn't doing this anymore, and in the summer of 2000, she ended the marriage.

I moved back to the dorms and started dating another woman who had just been reassigned to Vegas from Korea where she had saved a lot of money. I decided I wanted to help her spend it all. We gambled, drank, and went to strip clubs. A year later, the Air Force prosecuted me for spending up to $30,000 of her money. She claimed I stole it, but I really just convinced her to let me spend it. I was sentenced to the Air Force jail in Vegas. They transferred me to jail in Albuquerque, New Mexico. I got to see my son before I left. He was nine months old. I gave him a hug and a kiss and handed him back to his mom. I spent five months and twenty days in jail on that sentence. On December 15, 2000, the Air Force kicked me out of the military. My plan was to go back to Vegas, and where I thought I would start a life and raise my son. The Air Force told me I could stay in the base hotel for $8 a day. I decided to stay for a month to figure out my life. I flew back to

The Furthest Distance Between Two Points

Vegas for one day. Then, the military changed their mind and kicked me off base, so I left. My grandfather contacted a truck driver friend of his who trucked me back to Tulsa, Oklahoma, and that was it.

I left my son and ex-wife and moved back to Tulsa.

My Unfulfilled Promise to Change

Six days after I moved back, I started using drugs for the first time since that day in Oklahoma City in the bathroom of the brewery. I was working two jobs and living with a woman when I met a young lady who would be my future daughter's mom. She waited tables, and I cooked. One day, I made a joke to her. She messed up an order, and I got the order out and said, "Well, if I get the order out, you owe me a kiss." We hit it off, and we went out that night. After a few weeks, I moved out with the girl I was living with and moved in with her. She had a nine-month-old son, whom I later considered one of my own. His dad signed over his rights, and her parents were taking care of the baby. We worked hard, played hard, and did some drugs together. It was nothing crazy, but we did a lot of drinking and going out at night. We had a fun relationship. Then she got pregnant three months after we were together.

We moved into a rent house and got married. I stopped doing a lot of drugs. Minus a few times on scattered weekends, I had dropped the drugs whenever she and I started dating. However, I began working at a second restaurant for a guy who was a complete drug addict. A few months before my daughter was born, I started doing a bunch of cocaine again. The drug use got out of hand. I stayed up for days at a time and didn't go home.

I remember the day my daughter was born. I remember everything clearly. I was sober. On January 12, 2004, we had this beautiful little girl. The nurses took her to the nursery so her mom could get some rest. One of them asked if I wanted to feed my daughter. I told her I absolutely wanted to feed my daughter. I had never fed a baby. That's because I wasn't involved in my oldest son's life. I sat in the nursery and fed my baby girl. I just sat there. I'm not exactly sure how long I held her. I just know that family members were standing there knocking on the nursery door, wanting to see more of her. I sat there for hours talking to her. I swore I was going to change my life. I was going to be a good father and be responsible and do the right things and not screw this up like I did with my son. That's why, a week before my daughter was born, I stopped drinking and doing drugs.

My wife and I worked alternating schedules. I worked at a popular Asian chain restaurant as a cashier. I quit the job where I was doing drugs and poured all my effort into this new restaurant. My wife worked nights and was finishing nursing school. We were both busy, and I started talking to other girls. I worked all the time and got promoted to the assistant manager job. She became a stay-at-home mom, working a couple shifts here and there. I eventually got promoted to general manager. The money was really good. We weren't doing much as a couple. I was always talking to somebody else, always doing something else, always going out, drinking, and eventually doing drugs again. I was irresponsible. I wasn't a good father. I wasn't a good husband.

Our daughter was super colicky, but my mother-in-law was extremely helpful. I remember one night calling my mother-in-law because our daughter would not stop crying, and my wife was at work. I just needed some help. I asked her if she could come over. So, she did. I handed my daughter to her grandmother, who kindly asked if I wanted to leave for a little while. I did. I left and went to the bar.

I wasn't willing to be responsible for my family, which is so ironic because I was responsible professionally. I made work my number one priority and strived to be the best I could be at my job, but I had no desire to be the best husband, the best father, or even a good person. I excelled at everything except for the things that really matter. Because of my work ethic, management came to me and showed me their plan to open a store in Oklahoma City, then in Edmond, and then return to Tulsa to open two more stores. They offered me the opportunity to open new restaurants and eventually manage all six stores in Oklahoma. My wife and I went to Oklahoma City to look at houses. We put a deposit down to rent a really nice home in Edmond. She would attend the University of Oklahoma to finish her nursing degree, and I would open the new restaurants. Life would be great. Looking back, I realize I thought like an addict, "We just need to change the scenery and do something different, and that will fix it all." About a week before we were supposed to move, I stayed out all night and all day doing cocaine with some guys, and I didn't go home.

My wife told me she's not moving. She's not doing this. She told me I needed to get sober, stay in Tulsa, and work there. We had a lot of family and support there. My boss offered me a $30,000 raise to move to Edmond, so I took the money, left my wife, the son I considered my own, and my daughter, and relocated to Edmond alone.

Professionally, I was living a dream at 25 years old, making a hundred thousand dollars a year. I was the boss of over a hundred people, and our restaurants excelled in revenue and customers. The company started copying what we were doing and implementing our strategies across the rest of the locations. I didn't take a day off for over six weeks. I talked to my wife a couple times and told her I would start taking off on Tuesdays and Wednesdays and go in on Thursday afternoons to be with the kids. So, we agreed to meet halfway between Tulsa and Edmond. We started communicating more, and I was present with my kids, going on playdates and spending time at the park. I was becoming a real father to my kids.

On July 4th, I went to Tulsa to watch fireworks with my family. My wife and I stayed up and talked all night, trying to figure out how to make us work. We loved each other. All I needed to do was quit doing drugs. I promised her I would do it, and she agreed to move to Edmond for the remainder of the time I had left there. Then, we would move back to Tulsa. I drove back to Edmond. She was supposed to arrive the following weekend. I went out instead. I didn't answer her calls. I got high all weekend and spent the weekend with a couple different girls. And that was it.

Loss of Hope

I broke my promise to my wife, and I broke my promise to my daughter. From that point on, there was no reason for me to ever be sober. I wasn't seeing my kids anymore. I wish I could say she pulled them from me, but she didn't. I didn't make them a priority. I started doing cocaine every single day. I was making really good money, living a crazy life fueling my cocaine habit, yet still working

The Furthest Distance Between Two Points

12 to 14 hours a day, seven days a week. I had connections in the Oklahoma City/Edmond area and unlimited access to cocaine, so I would go out, get high, and end the night with $500 bar tabs. That's when I started stealing from my employer.

For months, I manipulated deposits and credit cards and hid company money. One day, my assistant manager called me and said, "There's something that doesn't make sense on the deposit." I responded, "Oh, yeah." And he said, "What's going on?" I said, "Oh, that's me. I have all that money." And he shockingly replied, "What?" I said, "Yeah. I'm going to bring you my keys and card, and I will call our boss." Stunned, he responded, "What are you talking about, Josh?" I said, "That money that's missing, it's me."

And so, I called my boss on the way to work, and I said, "I've stolen a whole bunch of money, I'm going to drop my keys and card off at the store with the assistant manager, and you let me know what you all want to do." He said, "What do you mean, Josh?" I told him, "I've stolen a bunch of money, and you guys haven't caught it. I got tired of it, so here you go." I got tired of moving all the money around and didn't want to do it anymore.

I left there and went and bought a bunch of liquor, some beer, and cocaine and had a bender for four days. I knew I was for sure going to jail over this. I already had a misappropriation charge with another restaurant I worked for before this one. I borrowed money from the safe with permission from my boss and then paid it back with paychecks. The problem is you can't borrow a corporation's money. We were audited, and there was an "IOU" in the safe from me for $1,200. I used money I didn't have permission to use. Because of the charge, I was on a two-year deferred sentence. I just finished my community service and paid my fines. I had 15 days left on the sentence, and the conviction would have disappeared. I knew I was going to prison. This was the exact same thing I did for the second time. There was no way I was getting out of this.

My boss called and told me they talked about it, and they didn't want to ruin my life. He said, "Josh, you seem to be doing a great job of that all by yourself. You know what you could become and what you could do if you would just get your life together. You've made us so much money, and you're so good at this. So, here's the agreement: if you tell us what you did and how you did it because we can't figure out where all the money is, and you sign over your last check and bonus check, we will not prosecute you." They accounted for $18,000, but the total was over $50,000 in approximately six months.

I was making over a hundred thousand dollars a year and now I was back living with my grandma and grandpa. Again, I swore that I was going to get my life together. But I didn't. I ended up in jail for thirty days. I don't even remember why. Being thrown in jail became my norm. I can't even count how many times I've been arrested or all the reasons I've been arrested for, but I always managed to talk my way out of what I had done, and most of the time, I was able to get the charges lessened to a deferred sentence. Jail was no big deal. I was arrogant. I knew I could get out of any charge. In 2008, I was charged with home repair fraud and would end up in jail again.

This time, I didn't have the money to bond out, so I sat in jail for a while until I pleaded my case to a judge who put me on probation. I got out of it once again.

The Furthest Distance Between Two Points

There's no way to summarize the next few years of my life. They were complete chaos and madness, and I went completely off the rails. I was doing drugs, drinking a lot, drinking and driving a lot, and sleeping with a bunch of random women. As much as I don't want to admit it, having sex with a bunch of women, chasing money, and gambling with zero responsibilities was a lot of fun. I'm a high-intensity guy. I would pass out after binging on alcohol and then wake up and drive home. I liked the chaos. But even with all the excitement, I could not fill this feeling of emptiness that I had. So, I kept going for more. From 2008 until 2013, being in and out of jail and bouncing from place to place was my life.

I got a job at a fast-food restaurant because they would pay weekly. A guy was going to let me stay with him. He had an extra room. It was him and his brother. But his brother knew I was a drug addict, and his brother said, "No, this isn't going to happen." I remember sleeping on his porch one night because I kept knocking on the door, and he never opened it. The next day, I said, "Man, what happened?" He responded, "Oh, yeah. We weren't home." I knew he was lying because he didn't want me to stay with him. I literally had nowhere to go.

I reached a point where no one would answer the phone anymore. A hotel was being remodeled across the street from where I was, and there was a Conex box there, so I slept behind that Conex box for four days. I had been somewhat homeless for a long time because I was always staying at somebody else's place, or I would pay for a hotel for a week out of a paycheck. The last time I had a home was in 2006, when I lived in Edmond. But this time, I was truly homeless. I had a bag of clothes with four shirts, two pairs of jeans, and a pair of basketball shorts, and a Gizmo stuffed animal that one of my mom's friends gave me for my 5th birthday, the year my dad didn't get me anything. I slept outside on the ground with no place to go.

Then I got sick. I had to have my gallbladder removed. The doctor made a mistake and caused bile to dump in my insides. I had to have emergency surgery at another hospital, which forced me to stay in the hospital for a couple weeks. I lost 70 pounds. I would walk around for a few minutes and then go back to sleep for 10 hours because my body was shutting down. I almost died.
Two weeks after being homeless, in the hospital, and almost dying, I got a paycheck from a new job at another restaurant. Instead of paying rent or getting groceries, I cashed it, bought alcohol, drank until I passed out, and started doing drugs again. I snorted as much as I possibly could to see what would happen.

And nothing did. I didn't die. And I didn't find life. Instead, I chose to live in hopelessness and despair because I didn't think my life had any more value than that. At this point, I had fathered two children and considered another one my own, but I had never been involved in any of their lives. I had every opportunity financially through the restaurant business to succeed, but I squandered it all on drugs and alcohol. I could have had a great marriage, but I chose to chase other women. I could have had a great relationship with my family, but I chose to lie. I had every opportunity to have lived a life of freedom, but instead, I chose to stay chained to the addiction.

3

WHAT LIES BENEATH

The drugs, alcohol, women, and gambling were all a cover-up. They were symptoms of my disease, which stemmed from unworthiness, poor self-esteem, and abandonment. I had buried years of hurt and pain in my life, and because I didn't address the root cause of them, my issues went unresolved. It's like when you throw dirty clothes in the closet and keep throwing more dirty clothes on top of them. All the wounds from growing up were hidden deep inside of me. I never addressed the underlying issues, so I continued to make decisions to hide and avoid the pain. I slept with women so I wouldn't be alone. I self-medicated with drugs, alcohol, sex, lying, and other destructive habits to cover my lack of self-worth and all my insecurities.

I would get a job and make a ton of money, and everybody would think everything was great. "Oh, this guy's such a high performer; he's so fantastic. He's so well-spoken and dresses well." When in reality, my hidden pain and hurt are what actually drove me to look successful in the world's eyes. I was a top performer in everything I did. I had a consistent paycheck. I had a place to live. I worked hard. I excelled at salesmanship. The high performance covered up a lot of my deficiencies, including alcoholism and drug abuse. Because I was so good at what I was doing, I learned if I did an amazing job, nobody cared about anything else.

The Furthest Distance Between Two Points

What I was really doing was covering up my lack of self-confidence and self-esteem, which stemmed from what I believed about myself. These lies revolved around my dad leaving and my mom's demand for perfection and excellence that nothing I did was ever good enough and were further reinforced by the girlfriends who cheated on me.

LIE: I'm not good enough.
WHY: Because nothing I ever did was right.

LIE: I am less than.
WHY: Because I need to be better.

LIE: Nobody cares.
WHY: Because I was abandoned.

LIE: I'm not worthy enough for anyone to love me.
WHY: Because everyone left.

As time passed, these lies that started as a little four-year-old boy grew deep roots. They constantly looped in my head. I not only believed them, but they became a part of who I was. What I eventually realized is all the lies pointed to one big lie.

"This is all I'm ever going to be: a failure and a loser. It's who I am. I can't overcome this place in life." There was no way out because there was no other way. And I believed it. I was stuck in a destructive hamster wheel of life.

PART 2
TO SOBRIETY AND SUCCESS

4

TURNING TURMOIL INTO TRUTH

On February 14, 2013, I decided I would make a change. I moved halfway across the state with a buddy of mine to Duncan, Oklahoma. "Things will be different," I thought. "I am going to start new." I got a job and started working. However, my new life didn't last long. I drove to a bar in my friend's truck one day after work. I did what I had done so many other times. I got drunk and then started driving home.

That's when I saw the blue lights.

I didn't want to go to jail. So, I ran, but not on foot. I led the police in a high-speed chase through Stephens County. I sped down back roads, swerved on gravel roads, and drove across farms and ranches. I got away from the police that night.

But not for long. They put a warrant out for my arrest for knowingly endangering others while eluding a police officer's arrest. A few weeks later, on April 12th, I was arrested at work while waiting tables at a local Mexican restaurant and thrown in jail.

I did not walk out of that jail until March 6, 2014. I was there for almost a complete year.

The Furthest Distance Between Two Points

Stephens County jail was different from any other jail I experienced. The longest period of time I had spent in jail awaiting trial prior to this one was my time spent in jail in the Air Force. The Air Force was laid back in comparison to civilian jail. All the other times I went to jail, I was only there for a few days to a couple of weeks. I knew my stay would be short. I knew I would get out of jail.

This time, I knew I couldn't beat this charge. I had no one to come bond me out and sign for my release, and no bondsmen would let me out on bail. They didn't know me. I didn't have any property in town or any reason for them to set me free. After all the probation I had been on before now, there wasn't any chance I would go home a free man. So, I sat there in jail waiting as court date after court date got postponed. I knew that whenever I left that jail in Stephens County, I was going to state prison.

If you've been in jail, you know there's not a lot to do there. Some prisoners sleep as much as they can. Others play spades or dominoes or watch TV. There's a lot of time to try and fill up throughout the day. I don't know why I decided while sitting in the Stephens County jail cell to make the commitment I made. Maybe it was for something to do. Or maybe something inside me prompted me to pick up the book. But for whatever reason, I decided to read through the Bible from beginning to end; from Genesis to Revelation.

My Transformation

As I read John chapter five in the New Testament, something deep inside me stirred. In the story, Jesus Christ is walking through Jerusalem for one of the Jewish festivals and meets a man who had been sick for thirty-eight years lying next to the pool of Bethesda in town. Hundreds of people who were lame, blind, and paralyzed would lie by the pool, waiting for what they believed was an angel to stir the pool. The first person who could get into the pool after the waters moved would be cured of whatever disease they had. As Jesus is talking to the man, he asks the man if he wants to get well. The man makes a bunch of excuses. "Sir," the lame man replied, "I have no one to help me into the pool when the water is stirred. While I am trying to get in, someone else goes down ahead of me." The man is telling Jesus that he's been unable to walk for his whole life, so he can't get up, walk, or do anything for himself. He also complains that he doesn't have anyone to help him get in the water.

As I read this, all I kept thinking was, "Goodness gracious, this sure sounds a lot like me. I'm just complaining about who I am, where I am, that I can't get out of this situation, and no one wants to help me. I'm just stuck like this." I had a lot of excuses for where I was.

I could feel God's presence as I read Jesus' words in John 5:6, "Do you want to get well?" This feeling came over me, this desperation.

I verbally answered, "YES! I do. Yes, I do." I began to weep. I hit my knees, and I just cried out to Jesus. I said, "Yes. Yes, I want to get well. I'm so sick and tired of being sick and tired. I'm tired of being in and out of jail. I'm tired of being in and out of rehab, from couch to couch, here and there, kicked out, homeless, and living the madness that I created for myself. Yes, I want to get well!"

Right there, in THAT moment, something unbelievable happened to me. I can only liken it to what happened to a guy in the Bible when the scales preventing him from seeing the truth of who Jesus was instantly fell off his eyes. I felt this miraculous change in my heart and in my life.

The story of the lame man by the pool finishes with Jesus telling him to "Get up! Pick up your mat and walk." At once, the man was cured. He picked up his mat and walked.

I decided to pick up my mat.

I turned my life and heart over to God that day, and my healing process began. A passion for God's Word ignited inside me, like when I was 10. I fervently studied the Bible and talked to other guys in jail about Christ. Then something incredible happened. We started having Sunday afternoon church in Stephens County Jail. We turned our cell into a church, got some colored pencils and wrote Scriptures on the wall, and drew pictures to honor God.

Every day, I earnestly sought God. I began identifying and address-ing the root of my problems, allowing me to discover why I was choosing to act the way I was and why I chose such a destructive path. Amazing things began to happen. I started to heal. My life was transforming. I grew spiritually and emotionally. I wrote apolo-gy letters to people in my life who I hurt. I thanked them for what they did for me. It was really a different me. I felt different. I felt changed. I felt full of God's Spirit. I felt like God was going to take me to where he wanted to take me so long ago before I ran from him.

When I was in jail, some younger guys stole my commissary, which is the additional food and snacks you can pay for while in jail. Normally, when that happens in jail, the only option is to fight back. I chose not to retaliate. Instead, I chose to walk in the love of Christ. I let the words I was reading live in me, resulting in a change in my heart and my actions.

When the bad court news came, I stayed positive and enthusiastic. I continued to live how God instructs us to live. The jail saw the changes in me, too. I became a trustee, which allowed me to work outside the jail and receive special privileges. I slowly gained more and more freedom. When I got released in March 2014, I went to a sober living community run by a local church. I made a commitment. I would be involved in church and strengthen my relationship with Jesus. February 14, 2013 was the last day I did any drugs.

But even though my relationship with Jesus grew, and I tried hard to make good choices, I never stopped drinking.

A Change in Choices

The continued drinking kept me frequenting bars and dance clubs. One day, after playing a round of golf with a friend and his girlfriend, we decided to go to the Hall of Fame, a local dance club where they played country music and live bands performed. That's where I met Amy.

My friends and I were taking shots and drinking beer when I saw Amy and her friends at the table next to us. I walked up to Amy and said, "Hey, let's dance." She looked me up and down, staring at my flip-flops, golf shorts, and polo, wondering who this guy was who wasn't wearing boots, jeans, or a button-up shirt. I could tell she was thinking that this was not the most country attire in a two-stepping dance bar. I confidently told her, "I dance better than every guy in this bar." She agreed to dance with me. We danced to the Garth Brooks song, "Rodeo." She got onto me for doing all the "spinny stuff." We danced that night and then went to a nearby local casino and hung out late into the night.

After that, we started talking. A couple weeks later, Amy told me she wasn't interested in a relationship. She didn't want to be involved with anyone, so she was going to be done with whatever we had.

That was in late July, and I couldn't get her off my mind. She was different than anyone I had ever been with or dated. I called her one night, and I told her I wasn't going to let her get rid of me. She said she didn't really have time, but after talking for a little while, she said, "Fine, I have tickets to Gary Allan." So, for our first real date, we went to dinner and a Gary Allan concert. I didn't have much money. I didn't have more than $100 to my name. I didn't have any transportation, and I was living in a sober living community called Wings of Freedom.

She picked me up for our date, and we went to El Chico for dinner. They had a $5.99 enchilada special, which was perfect because that was about all the money I had with me. That was August 30, 2014. Sitting there at dinner, I told her everything about my past.

I told her about my children.

I told her about the drug and alcohol abuse.

I told her about my promiscuity.

I told her about the number of times I'd been in jail.

I told her about all the felony convictions I've had.

I told her about the money I owed the IRS and the money I owed the court system. I told her I hadn't been a good person up to that point in my life, and I had recently gotten out of jail in March. We sat there, and I spent twenty minutes telling her everything I had done wrong, everything I was, everything I had been, and she didn't get up and leave. I later found out that Amy used to work at a jail I frequented, the Rogers County Jail in Oklahoma. I also found out later that Amy's never done any drugs, never smoked a cigarette, never ran around with men, and had only been drunk a couple of times in her entire life.

We finished dinner, went to the concert, and then went dancing. Shortly after, Amy and I moved in together. But I kept drinking. I went to work, came home, and drank Bud Light and Jagermeister with Red Bull until I passed out every night, Monday through Sunday. The pattern of my life remained the same.

Until Amy drew the line.

On December 8, 2015, we attended Amy's company Christmas party, and I had too much to drink. The next day, on December 9, 2015, Amy told me she had enough.

The Furthest Distance Between Two Points

"I'm done," she said. "I'm not going to live like this anymore. I'm not going to do it." She was sick of it.

For years, Amy dealt with a bad marriage. She waited to divorce her ex-husband after the kids left home. She had already been through a difficult relationship. She didn't need another one.

She said, "I'm not going to kick you out on the street. That's not what I want for your life." That's the kind of person Amy is. She wouldn't kick me out with nowhere to go. She told me I could sleep in the other room and take a couple weeks to find a place, then get my stuff and leave.

I stood there facing the second most important decision in my life after choosing to follow Jesus.

That day in December, I had to make a choice. I could choose to keep drinking and lose everything important to me, or I could give up the alcohol and keep the one woman I remained faithful to and whom I loved. Like many addicts, there were so many times in my life when I claimed to be sober. Fifty. That's the number of times I attempted to get sober. They were always for short periods of time, and often, my motives were to stay sober long enough for someone to not be mad at me. I had been at this crossroads before, choose my family or choose my addictions. This time, I made the right decision.

I walked to the kitchen sink and poured out the alcohol. I got rid of it all.

I looked at her and made another commitment. "I'll never drink again. I'm done." And that was it. December 9, 2015, is my actual sobriety date.

I was done. I was tired of losing people in my life. I always chose what I wanted. I had to break the pattern. Every time I started to make the right decision, I eventually chose me again. I received ultimatums before from family, friends, and ex-wives. "If you don't stop doing cocaine…" I responded by doing more. "If you don't stop drinking…" I drank more. My daughter and son's mom told me to stop chasing money. We didn't need any more. I moved to Edmond and took the raise. With every ultimatum, I always rebelled against it. This time, I did not want another relationship to be ruined by my negative decisions. I didn't want to hurt Amy anymore. I just couldn't bear to break another woman. And I loved her. I finally understood the love of God when I quit running from him. I finally knew what real love was. Real love is what God has for me unconditionally. I was able to love because I understood love. I knew I loved Amy with a passion and a desire that I never ever thought I could. And I couldn't bear to lose her.

To this day, I don't know why Amy stayed. There is no rational, logical reason why she would have. When she met me, I lived in a sober living house, and I had no car. On our first date, I told her what a mess I made of my life and all the problems I had, and I was drunk every night of the week for months. But Amy stayed and decided to walk out my sobriety with me. I joined Celebrate Recovery and was able to go through their step-study program. Amy was there through every single step of it. If you've ever had a loved one in recovery or gone through recovery yourself, you know it's not an easy process or a simple road to accept. There's a lot of pain, a lot of heartache, and a lot of things that you must go through to get to the other side of an addiction.

When I made that decision to get sober, I decided to be a better person and to live a better life. I focused on the discipline I learned as a child and what that means. Discipline is choosing what you have to do versus doing what you want to do. And Amy was there. She chose to go through the difficult process of my healing. The recovery program opened all my past wounds and pain and made me face all the horrible choices I made in my life. Until then, I never processed through any of it.

Amy stuck with me every single day. She loved me every day. She was there for me every day. She was the rock in my life that I needed. God knew I needed her. As I started to get healthy, I began to understand God's plan for my life. He had already laid out his plans. I just didn't know him enough to follow them. I was never supposed to walk this path of death and destruction. God always wanted me to walk with him, and follow him, and chase the greatness he had for me.

God also taught me that I'm his child. That's who I am. I'm God's child. He is my Father. He is the one who guides and directs me. He is the one who I turn to for encouragement and correction. He is the one who will love me unconditionally regardless of what I've done. He is the one who will never leave me or forsake me.

I've been asked multiple times why I finally chose to give up my addiction. Love is the most powerful force in the world. Love had to be the driver. I loved Amy like I've never loved anyone in my life. I wasn't willing to lose her. I loved her that much. I could lose everything in my life; just give me Amy. It's the love that God has for us. Not only did I understand God's love for me, but I was overwhelmed by it, which allowed me to pour out the same indescribable love for Amy. It's a love that you cannot quantify.

I proposed to Amy in December 2016, and we were married on November 21, 2017.

Choosing Amy meant I was choosing to live. I tattooed Deuteronomy 30:19 on my chest. "This day I call the heavens and the earth as witnesses against you that I have set before you life and death, blessings, and curses. Now choose life, so that you and your children may live." Choosing life means living life more abundantly, choosing positivity, and choosing discipline. I wanted something more for my life than what I had done for the past years. I wanted a different life. One life-giving choice led to another, which led to another, which led to thousands of future God-centered choices, including my decision to lay my cigarettes down at the altar. Literally.

One Sunday, our pastor preached a message about taking something we were dealing with and nailing it to a physical cross standing in the front of the church. He had the congregation write down whatever we needed to give to Jesus on a white piece of paper. He gave us a nail and a hammer, and we were to literally nail it to the wooden cross, giving it to Jesus so that his blood, which was shed on the cross by nails, would cover and take away whatever was on that paper. I thought about what I needed to nail to the cross. I quit drinking. I quit doing drugs. I wasn't sleeping around with women. But I was still smoking. Standing there, I thought, "It's really hard to tell somebody about God when you're standing there smoking a cigarette. You've got a great relationship with God, but you still need a substance to help you. Not only do you smoke cigarettes, but you smell like them too." I felt convicted, like someone was tugging at me. I knew it was God. It was time to quit smoking. The worship team started singing, and as the people praised and worshiped Jesus, I walked up to the altar and laid down my cigarettes at the foot of the cross. It was December 2016, and I never smoked another cigarette again. However, even though I felt the release from the addiction to cigarettes, I didn't allow myself to walk away from the nicotine. I chose to pick up vaping.

Vaping was the one thing preventing me from the power of God's glory in my testimony. I found myself trying to talk to someone about what God has done in my life and trying to explain God has the power to help overcome drug and alcohol addiction while I was standing there vaping. I recognized that I wanted a better life, and I wanted all of what God has for my life, and part of getting there was deciding to quit hanging on to my security blanket. I was like Linus in the cartoon Peanuts. I was still relying on something other than God. This time, it was vaping. I wouldn't let it go.

Growing up, I had two best friends, Chris and Sean. Mr. Claybon is the father of Chris. He and Sean's dad, Mr. Highberger, were two influential men in my life who were like father figures to me. One of the things I always remember is that both dads were always home for dinner. Anytime I would go over for dinner, they were always there. They were always present. Mr. Claybon used to say to me all the time, "How is that working out for you, Josh?" I would argue about whatever topic we were discussing, and he would finally say, "How is that working out for you?" He knew the decisions I was making needed some dramatic changes if I wanted to make a dramatic change in my life. My mom did, too. She used to say to me, "If you want to change, do something different." Those conversations kept repeating in my head. I knew if I kept doing things the way I was doing them, nothing was ever going to change, including vaping.

God started my journey to a transformed life with "Do you want to get well?" It all starts with these four words: Do you want to? Do you want to have a successful marriage? Do you want to have happy relationships in life? Do you want to work out? Do you want to get healthy? Do you want to quit doing drugs? Do you want to quit drinking? Do you want to stop vaping?

It seems so trivial, but it is a fact. Anything you want to do starts with "do you want to?". The people who make it to the other side are those that want to.

For me to be successful in business, have a healthy marriage, have a healthy relationship with my business partner, pour into others' lives, and be willing to give financially, spiritually, and emotionally, it's because I want to. It's a simple want to. You have to want it more than what you currently are doing.

So, I quit. I stopped vaping cold turkey. I threw it in the trash. I wanted to quit because my want was what God wanted. He wanted all my dependency to be on Him. So, I surrendered my want to His.

Another Surrender

Amy and I were doing well. We bought a home and started saving money. I was working for a gentleman installing sprinklers, but we felt it was time to step on a new path and make a difference. On Monday, May 8, 2017, we started a small business called Living Water Irrigation. We quickly added two partners, Pedro, and Jesus Vargas. My mom loaned me $5,500 to buy my first work van. I told her I would pay her back with interest. We picked up the van in Muskogee, a little town outside of Tulsa. It wasn't extravagant, but it was all I needed to begin the journey. Mom also went to the supply house with me in Tulsa and loaned me $2,300 to buy the parts and tools I needed. The "company" was a shovel, a bunch of sprinkler heads, and me. I called everyone I knew on the way to and from Muskogee. I told them I had just quit my job and started a sprinkler company, so if they knew anyone who needed sprinkler systems or sprinklers fixed, please give them my information because I really needed the work. By the time I got back to Tulsa, we had eight service calls and three installations.

The first couple of installs were friends helping me by giving me business. I don't even know if they really wanted the system, but they bought it from me. We had work on Tuesday and Wednesday and then on Friday and Saturday.

But Thursday morning, we had no work. Nothing. I had nothing to do. I didn't want Amy to know, so I got up and drove to Davis Supply in Tulsa. I sat in the parking lot because they weren't open yet. It was five o'clock in the morning. As I sat in my car staring at the closed sign, all these thoughts flooded my head. "What have I done? I left a job making $80,000 a year, and now we started this business, and we have bills to pay, and we just bought a house, and I don't even have work to go do. What have I done? This is the dumbest thing I ever could have done in my whole life. Amy had all this confidence in me, and I failed on day three." I sat in my car and cried. I begged God for help. Then, as clear as day, I heard the voice of God. "Get up and do something about it." God told me to take action. By that time, they were open. I had been crying for a while. I went inside and got a case of rain sensors that tell a sprinkler system to shut off during or after a rainstorm, and I knocked on doors all day until I sold all the rain sensors. And I said I'll never, ever again give into fear or pity or doubt. Never.

At the most stressful point in my life, I had to decide whether to follow what God said and act or give in to the pressures of life. What I later realized was that the real choice was finally deciding to surrender my will to God's. Surrendering to God means giving up what you want now for what God wants most for your life. I had to lay down my will and give up my wants. The decision to choose God happens in all areas of life and is a daily choice. Whether it be refraining from drinking too much Dr. Pepper or stopping what I am doing to help the person God placed in front of me at that moment, I have a daily choice to follow what God wants me to do.

Jesus modeled complete surrender to God when he made the decision to willingly be crucified on the cross to save all of us. It was his choice. He said yes to God, his Father. He said yes to sacrificing his life in exchange for ours. Jesus died to wipe away our sins. That's full surrender. That's a complete trust that God knows better than us. And he does. God knows the plans that he has for us, and those plans are not to harm us but to give us hope and a future and help us prosper. God showed me through Celebrate Recovery that not only is he my heavenly Father, but I can always trust him. God's ways are better than my ways. His choices are perfect. Mine are flawed.

The Furthest Distance Between Two Points

To choose Jesus' way instead of my own required humility. I recognized I needed him. I've always been good at sales, but as I relied on him, he took what I'm best at and said, "I'll show you how I can do it better." And he did. He continues to give me the strength and power to do more than I can possibly imagine. And he works this way with everything in my life. Once I fully decide to give 100% of my life and my decisions to him, I tapped into his power instead of my own. Anytime I try to do anything with my own strength, it fails. Whether it's in my business, my life, my marriage, or my relationships, anytime I'm not listening to God or walking with love for others, or not making sure that the things I'm doing are led by him, it never works. So, I choose Jesus—today and every day.

I worked seven days a week, from sunup to sundown. I did whatever it took to survive. I got up in the morning around 4:00 am and planned my day. By the time I left, I knew what I was going to do with the day, where I needed to be, and what jobs were priority.

I would leave the house and work all day and then come home at dark and take a shower. When I got out of the shower, Amy would have two turkey sandwiches with Wavy Lay's potato chips and a glass of milk waiting for me. I'd give her a kiss, sit down, eat the sandwiches and chips, drink the milk, and go to bed. Then, I would get up and do it all over again.

Three weeks into business, I got a phone call from a gentleman named Josh. He called me and said, "Hey man, I hear you're hungry." And I said, "Excuse me?" He said, "I heard you're hungry. You just started a sprinkler company, right?" I said, "Yes, sir." He said, "Well, my name's Josh. I got your number from the supply house. I got this job that another guy was going to start, and if you want it, you can have it. You just have to be able to start it on Monday."

I met him at his job, and he showed me the install plans. I told him I needed the evening to think about it and would call him in the morning. That evening, I met with Pedro and Jesus at their house. We sat down at the kitchen table and rolled out the set of plans. We were in way over our heads. It was just the three of us, and this was a monster commercial job that typically companies with a ton of experience and a ton of equipment and logistical help and support would've done, but we decided we would do it. I called Josh the following morning and told him, "We're in. We'll do the job."

After that, I called Ditch Witch and spoke to Andy in sales. We didn't have any money. I asked him, "Is there any way you guys could figure out something to get me a trencher? I just committed to this job, and I don't have any money to buy one." They were able to work out a deal for me on a long-term rental. We've been loyal to them ever since. They've always taken great care of us.

We also didn't have a trailer. I called a guy who wanted some work done. He told me he had an old landscape trailer. On a Thursday, we did the work for him and picked up the trailer. It was in bad shape. A friend of ours who owns a large welding shop agreed to fix the trailer for me at no charge. I dragged the trailer to his shop. Looking back, I know he and his guys spent a ton of money and time to get the trailer where we could use it.

On Saturday, we went to the supply house and filled the trailer with all the parts and tools we needed. We didn't have enough money, to purchase all the things we really needed, but we had enough to get started.

On Monday, we laid out the sprinkler system and started digging ditches. The job had to be done in three weeks. That was the deadline. We either finished the project by then, or we didn't get paid. We worked until dark every day. We hired a couple helpers to join us for the second week. They ended up becoming employees and have been with us ever since. My day began at the commercial job with the guys. I would leave to do a service call and then go back to work on the commercial job. I would leave again to do a presentation to a homeowner to sell another sprinkler system and then go back to the commercial job. I continued that routine, day after day.

On the weekends, Pedro, Jesus, and I would do additional installs for extra money to pay our helpers. We weren't paying ourselves anything because we needed helpers for the commercial job. Two weeks and four days later, we had the system running, and the customer signed off on our completion. We finished three days before the deadline. Unfortunately, that job almost ended our company. It took five months to receive payment. Ditch Witch wanted their money for their trencher, and Davis Supply wanted their money for the parts. Everybody was knocking on our door.

We made commitments based on us getting that done and based on us getting paid. But we honored our word and managed to get all our debts paid.

Over the next few years, the business grew. I left every morning before the sun came up, and I got home after dark. I was our service tech, our office person, our crew organizer, and our salesman, and I collected and deposited all the money. As we continued to grow, we hired our first employee. Her job responsibilities were to answer calls and perform clerical tasks. She did her job. She also took money from me.

Initially, I was extremely upset. But how could I be? I ripped off so many people in the past that I would be a hypocrite to go after her for what she owed me. I received grace for doing the same exact thing. So, I didn't do anything to try to collect. I left it alone. I responded the way the Bible tells us to respond. I extended the same grace that was given to me.

Growing the business wasn't easy. Building something from nothing requires a lot of consistency and hard work. Although we saw a 300% increase in revenue from 2017 to 2018, and we continue to trend upward every year, we had tough times. That morning, in the parking lot outside Davis' Supply store, I had a choice to make. I had to change my mindset because a lot of doors were slammed in my face that day. A lot of people cussed at me and wanted to run me off or call the cops. I knew if I wanted the business to succeed, I was going to have to overcome any doubts and fear. I changed the dialogue in my head from "I can't do this" to "I am the greatest salesman ever."I began reversing all the negative thoughts in my head with truths of who I was and who I knew I could become.

This morning, I woke up at 3:27 am. I had a small headache, and I was a little cranky. I went to the restroom and threw some water on my face. I prayed the same prayer I've prayed every morning for the past eight years, "Father, thank you for today. Thank you that I get to do this today. Please keep me sober, humble, and honest."

The Furthest Distance Between Two Points

I got to work at 4:15 am. Years ago, that's the time I went to bed after a night of drunkenness and drugs, or it's the time I took another hit of cocaine before work because I didn't go to bed that night. Now, I choose to be sober and honest. The choice isn't hard anymore, but it didn't happen overnight. Incremental changes occurred every single day for a very long time.

The transformation was not some huge, unbelievable, overnight miracle for me. God can do amazing things, and miracles happen every day. But for my life, I didn't go to bed one night and wake up the next day way better looking and no longer a drug addict like I was in a movie. I had to choose Jesus daily. I had to do it then, and I still do it today. Every day.

5

TWO CHOICES, INFINITE REGRETS

Two decisions altered the entire trajectory of the rest of my life, causing a domino effect of regrets. I shouldn't have gone to the brewery that day, and I should have gone to any other place in the world, as my grandfather told me to, besides Las Vegas, Nevada. If I removed these two pivotal choices and instead chose to work through the pain in my life, I believe I would have stayed on the right path the whole way. I could have been a good person. I could have been a good father. But I made the wrong choices. And now there are regrets.

If you regret one thing and you don't fix the problem, you wind up regretting the next thing. If you regret the next thing and continue what you are doing, you wind up regretting the next thing. It's a series of regrets. Regrets are interconnected. One is linked to the other that is linked to the other that is linked to the other. A regret results when we deflect the responsibility of choice.

My greatest regret is not having a relationship with my children.

The last time I saw my daughter was her fourth birthday at Chuck E. Cheese. She was excited to see me, her dad. I was so happy being there. But I was hungover. I had been out way too late the night before her birthday party. I never knew that would be the last day I saw her. Now I live with regrets.

I regret that my grandfather passed away when I was in jail, but it was my choice that put me there. I chose to run from the cops. I have no relationship with my son who was born on October 19th. But that was my choice. And now I live with regrets.

If you are unwilling to regret, you are unwilling to accept responsibility for the decisions, thoughts, actions, and choices you make. The unwillingness to face things is the biggest struggle of an addict. That's why it's so easy to say you have no regrets because then you don't have to face them. You don't have to accept the fact that what you did was wrong, who you are is wrong, what you said was wrong, and your actions are wrong. You don't have to own them. You don't have to live through the disappointment. It's so easy for an addict to run away from things. The reason why you can't be an addict and have a close personal relationship with Jesus Christ is because you are always trying to run away from everything. For an addict, meth, cocaine, heroin, pills, sex, pornography—I can continue going down the list—they are all coping mechanisms. The substances temporarily mask the pain instead of having to deal with it.

To have regrets, you must face what you've done wrong. You must be repentant, feeling sadness or disappointment over something that has happened or has been done. You repent because you regret what you've done. If you have no regrets, then you have no repentance. Until you truly regret your life decisions, you can't lament over them and move forward. Lament means to mourn. You are supposed to lament. Many of us are unwilling to mourn, especially men. I'm not talking about today's society and the demasculation of men, but as men, we are told not to cry. We're not supposed to talk about our problems. We lock up our hurt inside and cover it up because we are not supposed to have feelings or emotions. We don't address what got us there in the first place, making it convenient to bury everything we feel and ignore our regrets. In the step study program, when I began to list all the people I've wronged and all the things I had done wrong, I had to acknowledge the sadness and disappointment in myself and in what others felt towards me. I had a lot of repentance.

God's Saving Grace

So, how does Jesus Christ come in all this? If you don't have Jesus, you live without repentance, and you don't regret anything you've done because you don't take responsibility. If you are not lamenting things, you are not allowing Jesus to heal those parts in you and help you. When Jesus becomes the new filter, lamenting the destructive choices becomes a passionate mourning of grief, which leads to repentance and healing.

When I realized all the wrong things I had done and that Jesus still loves me, I had the revelation knowledge of the depth of what Jesus did on the cross.

Once you lay something down, you don't pick it back up again or linger there. Once you lay whatever you are holding on to down at the foot of the cross of Jesus, you must move on because you have been forgiven. Jesus canceled the charge of our legal indebtedness; he took it away by nailing it to the cross. He paid the debt of our sins that we owed. It's like standing in front of a judge with a list of all the things you've done wrong that should put you in jail for life, and then the person who loves you the most steps in and says, "I'll take the punishment for all his crimes. Wipe his record clean."

Even though I have all this money and all these nice things, and I get to do all this nice stuff, if I were to dwell on the fact that I don't get to see my children, I would physically, emotionally, and spiritually die under the weight of not having my kids in my life. I'm not exaggerating or being flippant about this. If I were to really think about the fact that I've gained all these other things and done all these other things and positively affected other peoples' kids, but I don't have a relationship with my own children, if I were to constantly dwell and lament on that, it would be crushing.

At times, we need to dwell on the revelation God gives us and meditate on what he tells us, but we're not supposed to stay in a position longer than necessary. God always wants us to move forward and grow closer to him, but we are often reluctant to leave where we are because moving forward means doing something unfamiliar. Our nature is to return to something we know. We can be comfortable or courageous, but we can't be both. People refuse to change because it's so much easier to stay the same than it is to change.

Ultimately, we have two choices: the pain of change or the pain of regret. We can't draw closer to God if we're running away from him or stuck on something, which means we cannot get stuck in the past. It's what happens in so many people's lives. It's a binding circle of addiction and negative actions. We say, "I shouldn't have done this. Oh well, I'm going to do it again because I already did it." We linger in that pain. We should have a passionate expression of grief and sorrow, but we shouldn't linger there. I absolutely regret that I snorted those two lines of cocaine. I must face the fact that I chose to go do cocaine rather than raise my daughter and my sons. It's something I live with every day. But I can't linger there because if I'm unwilling or reluctant to leave, I can never have the relationship God wants me to have with them now. I accept the consequences of my decisions, but I also live with the hope that God will restore those relationships. I went through repentance, disappointment, and sadness. But if I were to linger on in what I did, I would be unable to move forward.

Facing the Giants

There's pain that changes us, and there's pain that hurts us. I was hurt for so long because of my dad and past relationships with girlfriends who cheated on me with my best friends, but I finally reached a point in my pain where I realized I didn't want to be the way I was anymore. I didn't want to hurt the next person. I didn't want to disappoint the next person. I didn't want to have to continue to go back and repent and ask for forgiveness for the same thing over and over again. I got tired of repeatedly "getting sober" and then going back to my old ways.

The recovery was an extremely painful experience. I had to recognize and work through all my flaws, hurts, and pains and choose to face them head-on so that I could get healed and delivered. On Tuesday evenings, I started to regularly attend Celebrate Recovery, which is a Christian based 12-step recovery program. Choosing to go back every Sunday afternoon to a Step Study program, do it again, work on myself, address all the hurt, and spend time in communion with Christ to understand those pains was difficult.

The Furthest Distance Between Two Points

The process was worse than sitting in isolation in jail. In jail, time passed with me and a book to read. In Step Study, you dig to find the root of the problems, and as they begin to surface, you pull them out one by one. It's painful.

I was sitting with a young man who was seven days sober, and I was talking to him about wounds and scars and healing and finding the root of the problem. And he said to me, "Josh, you want me to be clean, and I'm still bleeding." So, I told him, "Let's close it up. Let's figure out how to stop the bleeding so we can prevent it from getting worse. Then, we can treat the wound. In time, the wounds will scab and scar, and you will be healed."

As we talked, I realized my bleeding started when I was 3 years old. That's when my dad left. I didn't close the wound, so the wound got bigger, and I bled more. God kept bringing "doctors" to my life to stop the bleeding. If you look at the father figures in my life, including my grandfather, all these people were trying to stop the bleeding. I never got a chance to get treatment or let the wound scar. I chose to keep bleeding. I was hemorrhaging for decades.

There's a story of a woman who had been bleeding for twelve years. She saw multiple doctors and kept getting worse. She heard about a man in town who could heal her. She thought to herself that if she could just touch his clothes, she would be healed. So, she fought through the crowd and touched his cloak. Immediately, her bleeding stopped, and she felt in her body that she was freed from her suffering. At once, the man realized someone had touched him and that power had gone out of him. He turned around in the crowd and asked, "Who touched my clothes?"

The people around him told him that there were a lot of people touching him. But the man kept looking around to see who had done it. Then the woman, knowing what had happened to her, came, fell at his feet, and, trembling with fear, told him the whole truth. He said to her, "Daughter, your faith has healed you. Go in peace and be freed from your suffering." The man the woman touched was Jesus.

When I said yes to Jesus in Stephens County jail, the bleeding stopped immediately. Then, I had to go through the healing process. Jesus didn't just die on the cross to conquer our sins and bring us peace, but he also died for our healing.

God took my loneliness and forced me to rely on his Son, Jesus Christ. I didn't realize until I was in the middle of recovery that there was this emptiness inside me. It's why I could never sleep alone and why I was always trying to find some woman because I felt so empty. I had a hole in my life from my dad leaving, which was exasperated by me being a poor kid who couldn't do anything right. As a kid, girls wouldn't talk to me, and boys made fun of me. I invited in any action that made me feel special. A woman willing to give herself to me and tell me that she loved me temporarily filled the void, and I masked the pain with substances. Relationships were of zero importance to me. I had no connection to anyone because I was never going to let anybody hurt me again. If a person didn't have sex, drugs, money, or something that served my needs, then I didn't have any time for that person.

As God helped me through the healing process, I also had to admit that my choices caused my pain and heartache. That's when I stopped blaming Satan for my problems and took responsibility for my decisions. I tell people all the time that Satan didn't really destroy me. I destroyed myself. God never intended for any of my pain to happen. Through prayer and meditation, I finally faced who I was so I could become who I am. I am approved and loved by Jesus. The freedom I received on the other side of going through all the pain is worth it. I don't care how much money I have now. I care about the freedom that I have. I can have a healthy relationship with my wife and not seek approval from other women. There's freedom in knowing that I have a real relationship with the woman I love and real relationships with my family and friends. I don't need anyone else's approval.

Recovery forced me to face my giants, but I didn't face them alone. I had God on my side. God promises to help us fight our battles. He knows the outcome because he already won. He claimed all-time victory when he died on the cross. It's like playing rock, paper, scissors and ALWAYS winning, except this time it's with giants and Jesus. Giants face Jesus. Jesus beats giants every time.

I still face giants today. They just change. I went through some of the loneliest times of my life for six years. There's no lonelier place than my office at 3:30 in the morning, trying to figure out how to inspire and motivate our team. How do I put on a positive face when I don't know how I'm going to make payroll? How do I fire the team up when somebody wrecks a brand-new truck and then somebody runs a trailer into another guy?

When I sit in my office in the mornings, and I'm not feeling it, like this morning, I spend time with Jesus. My drive this morning had no music, no podcasts, and no news. I was just talking to God. "God, I have a schedule to meet. I have things to do. I have a team to answer to. We have decisions that need to be made, and we have to grow." I now rely on God instead of others. I can tell you that sometimes it's still hard, and I still feel weak. I still have bad days. But there are so many things in my life that I can do now because I've been strengthened spiritually and emotionally. I've learned so much about myself and what I can go through and withstand. And I do it all sober.

When I started this book, the biggest giant in my life was that my mom had stage four cancer. We stood in the oncologist's office as the doctor delivered the news. Even though I'm 47, I'm still a 7-year-old kid at Mingo Manor Apartments with my mom. I've never lived without my mom. When we left the doctor's office, I realized that I couldn't buy my way out of this, and I couldn't work my way out of this. There's nothing I could do besides take my mom on her dream trips and love her. I didn't know how to navigate life without my mom.

The first thing my mom said to me when we got the diagnosis was, "I need to know. Are you going to go get loaded?" At the time, I was seven years sober. I said, "Nope, Mom, I'm going to go hit golf balls." She said, "Okay." And I lovingly repeated, "But I do need to go and hit some golf balls. Mom, I love you." So that's what I did. I got quiet with God and shed a lot of tears on the back of the golf range, hitting golf balls. I told God, "I don't know how to do this. I don't know what I'm supposed to do here." I heard him say, "Your mother is still here." I was overwhelmed with this unbelievable peace that flooded me on the north side of the Patriot Country Club. I couldn't fall again because she was still there. I wasn't going to make that my choice. I have a responsibility to cherish her legacy and all the commitment, sacrifice, and pain she went through to get me to today. I chose to value every moment, every conversation, and every day with her. I also chose not to let my mom's disease destroy what she built. My mom poured into my life to build Living Water Irrigation. I was not going to destroy the company or my life by making catastrophic choices because of her disease. I know I wouldn't be able to easily. I have the accountability of my wife and several men around me to stand firm, and I have a peace that only comes from my relationship with God. My confidence that I know I will make it through is not a confidence in me. It's a confidence in Jesus in me. I know I can't do this without the power of Jesus, and it's a peaceful place. After the diagnosis, my faith in God didn't waiver, and my behavior didn't change. I didn't revert to my old lifestyle. My mom's cancer was uncomfortable, but I chose to be courageous. I chose to remain sober and grow through the trial.

My mom died on September 21, 2023. At the time, this book wasn't complete. I was able to get her a rough draft, and in Debbi Wilson style, she had a lot of input. I've never done life without my mom. She was obviously my biggest fan, even when I was doing everything wrong. I was still her baby boy, and she still believed I was destined for greatness.

Because of the power of Christ in me and the people around me, I remained sober. I didn't realize my life was shaky until I had to face the biggest giant I've ever faced. I didn't realize that the choice to go back to my old life would stare me down in the mirror. Jesus is the only one who can transform Josh Wilson from shaky ground to a continued life of sobriety. God gets all the glory because it's not my power or strength that pulled me through my mom's death, but His.

You have to face your regrets, every single one of them, and be willing to lament, cry, wail, and accept the pain, the hurt, and the consequences that come alongside your decisions and choices. You have to understand what you did but not linger there. Don't get stuck in who you used to be, preventing you from becoming who God destined you to become. Don't be unwilling to move forward, or unwilling to do something different, or unwilling to get out of your comfort zone. So many of us feel like, "I'll never be anything but a drug addict." There was a long period in my life where I believed, "This is all I'm ever going to be." I was reluctant to leave because it was what was comfortable for me.

If you are willing to go through the process and choose to walk out all the pain and hurt it takes to go through a recovery program and face the root cause of your problem, with Jesus' help, you will get healed. The freedom that is on the other side is priceless. The only thing I wouldn't willingly give up right now is my sobriety and my relationship with Jesus Christ.

6
FORGIVENESS

After my dad disowned me and my brothers at age 10, I didn't speak to him again until I was 30 years old. By then, I had turned my life around and made some good friends, including my friend Nathan. During one of my conversations with Nathan, he encouraged me to reach out to my dad and try to forgive him to move past what happened. He said I needed to forgive him not only because unforgiveness is unhealthy but because my unforgiveness was holding me back from where I could be and where God wanted me to be. Nathan was right.

I knew my dad divorced his wife in Dallas and moved back to Tulsa. So, I called him. He picked up the phone, and I said, "You still play golf?" He said, "Yep." I said, "Great. I have a tee time at noon at Page Belcher Golf Course on Father's Day. If you would like to meet me there, great. If you don't show up, that's great too. It's up to you." I invited a friend. Just in case he didn't show up, I would press on, and we could still play golf. I didn't expect him to come.

Father's Day came, and my friend and I headed to the golf course. I was standing in the pro shop getting ready to pay for the rounds of golf, and I told the pro shop clerk I needed to pay for two at 12 o'clock for Wilson. I told him I didn't know if the third party was here yet. When we walked in, I saw a man standing in the shop.

The Furthest Distance Between Two Points

The man walked up to me and said, "Hey, Josh." It was my dad. I didn't even know it was him. I didn't recognize him. It had been twenty years. We shook hands and played golf. We talked. I told him I would like to try to rekindle our relationship and figure out how to get past what happened. We talked a few times after that, but he was unwilling to apologize for anything and own up to anything he did. I tried to have a relationship with him, but it never happened.

He moved away in 2011 to Wyoming. His sister Mary owned a large family oil and gas business, so he went to work for them. I didn't see him again until three years later, at his funeral. I was in jail when my grandfather died. My grandfather died on March 2, 2014. The funeral was on March 4, and I got out of jail on March 6. I missed it. My father died on March 13, 2014, one week after my grandfather. I didn't go to the funeral of the one man who impacted my life the most; instead, I attended the one man's funeral who caused me the most pain in my life.

My dad's nephew, John, was named after my dad. John and my dad were close. At the funeral, John walked up to me. "I'm really going to miss your dad," he said. I responded, "I wish I could say the same thing. You got to have a relationship with him. He got to raise you and hang out with you. I never knew him."

My dad is buried twenty tombstones down from my grandma and grandpa in Tulsa. My grandfather picked out a beautiful site. I go there occasionally, and sit under this beautiful tree, and play country music. One day, as I was leaning up against the tree and talking to my grandpa, I told him, "I need to walk over there and forgive my dad." And so, I did. I walked twenty tombstones over and sat down. I told my dad I knew he was a hurt little boy and didn't know any better. What my dad did was generational. His granddad left his kids, his dad left his kids, and he left us. He didn't know that there was anything different or search to find another solution or find another way. He didn't know Jesus, so he emulated what he saw. I told him I wished he would've gotten help and done something different, but I forgave him. I know it's not always that easy to forgive people, but for me, it was that easy.

I realized that if I ever wanted my kids to forgive me, I had to forgive my dad. I don't want at my funeral for the young man that I have a close relationship with who was born three years after my son on my son's birthday, to tell my son that he's going to miss me and for my son to respond, "I wish I could say the same thing. You got to have a relationship with him. He got to mentor you and hang out with you. I never knew him." If I ever want forgiveness for who I was and all the things I did to my children, my exes, my mom, my brothers, and everyone I hurt, if I ever want to get true forgiveness and move forward with my life, I can't have any unforgiveness. I had to release all the animosity and hurt so I could walk in what God has for me. God never intended for my dad to leave. So, I forgave him, and the result was immediate freedom.

Unforgiveness is destructive. Forgiveness is freedom. Forgiveness isn't saying what someone did to you was right. Forgiveness is releasing a debt that is owed to you. Jesus released our debt when he was crucified on the cross, and we were immediately forgiven. When you forgive, you also have to release that person from what they did or said. Often, we believe we forgave a person, but we never received freedom because we still hold on to the offense. When we let it go, it's like dropping one-hundred-pound weights on our shoulders that we have been carrying around for years. Years later, I realized that I truly did forgive my dad in the cemetery. I forgave him, but I never let the offenses go. We must ask ourselves what we are holding on to and harboring in our soul? Unforgiveness is the major contributor to alcoholism and drug abuse. When we forgive, we don't have to medicate anymore. The pain and hurt we have inside cause us to act out and root bitterness. Then we get stuck in a cycle that will only end when we forgive.

Looking back at my dad, I was angry for so long. I held onto so much hate and pain and anger. I was bitter that my mom had to teach me how to throw a football. I was bitter that I never got to learn how to weld, which is all his family does. I was angry that I never got to go fishing or do dad stuff with him. I had to let it all go. I couldn't willingly hate him anymore. I couldn't willingly sin anymore because hatred is a sin, and I hated him for walking out on us and how much my mom suffered. She worked so hard. He could have shown up for a few baseball games so she could nap. He could've paid child support or helped her so she wouldn't have had to work two jobs and go to school. I was angry at what he did to me and my brothers, but I hated him for what he did to my mom.

I held onto those emotions for years. I also held onto the Gizmo stuffed animal as a reminder that my dad didn't care. I chose to focus on all the negative thoughts and emotions towards my dad, and Gizmo reinforced the disappointment. At some point after being homeless, I lost Gizmo. I realize now that I needed to lose him. I had to let go of what he represented.

From age 10 to 30, I was so hurt by my dad that I was unwilling to pick up the phone and try to mend our relationship. Yes, he was my father, and he should have been the one to ask for forgiveness, but I could have easily forgiven him standing on that golf course at age 30. I tried to have a relationship with him, but the reality is I never forgave him. When I finally released everything and let all the negative emotions and thoughts go, God replaced them with joy, happiness, positivity, and optimism, and he gave me a future and hope. I traded my sorrows for joy.

Forgiven

When you start getting closer and closer to God, he reveals deep and hidden things, and sometimes, they aren't fun to hear. But he always knows what is best, so the hard truths are for our benefit. Even though I hated my dad for how he treated my mom, God revealed to me that I treated my mother way worse than my dad ever did. I remember she once asked me, "What would you do to a man who has treated me the way you treat me?" I quickly fired back, "I'd kill him." And she responded, "Well, then why do you do it?" Forgiving my dad wasn't the only forgiveness that needed to happen. I had to go to my mom and ask her to forgive me. I stole from my mom. I lied to my mom. I manipulated her and used the fact that she should help her little boy to get what I wanted. Repeatedly, I took advantage of her. I made empty promises to her after she bailed me out of jail, hired attorneys, and paid fines. I broke her heart hundreds of times. I was a horrible person to her.

But she forgave me just like she forgave my dad. Our relationship mended when I was in jail in Duncan, Stephens County. She drove six hours to see me, and we had a 30-minute visit. At the end of our conversation, she looked at me and said, "You're different."

The Furthest Distance Between Two Points

That's where our relationship started. I have not lied to my mom ever since.

I'm the fourth generation of Wilsons to leave their kids. The consequence of my choices is that I have no relationship with my three kids. I turned into my dad. My dad left because it's what his dad did. My dad modeled exactly what he saw. I did exactly what my dad did. I became that which I hated the most. I wasn't a dad. I described my dad to others as selfish. But I was selfish, too. No number of apologies, "I'm sorry," or "I didn't mean to do it," will ever make up for what was lost. I know personally how it feels because there's nothing my dad said when I reached out to him at 30 years old that ever made it right. I gave him a shot, but he chose not to fix what was broken. That's all I want. I just want a chance to be a dad. I screwed it up the first time, and now that they are grown, I just want a chance to prove to them that I'm not that same guy. I'm not selfish anymore. I just want to be a part of their lives.

But how do you go from not being a father at all to being one? I've had an infinite number of chances. I don't deserve another chance at all. I don't deserve my kids picking up the phone and saying, "Hey, I want to talk to you." I don't deserve it because I didn't live in a manner to earn it. Respect can't be demanded. It must be earned. I can't explain why that beautiful moment on January 12, 2004 in the hospital with my daughter didn't keep me focused on what matters. What do you say to your children when they ask you why they weren't worth you choosing them over alcohol, drugs, and sex? My brothers and I had the exact same conversations. Why didn't Dad care enough? Why are we not enough for him to be sober? And the answer is because I was so selfish, and I cared more about the things that don't matter than them. So, I pray for an opportunity to make it right with my three kids and to do what I should have done twenty-four years ago when my first son was born. Even at age 30, when I stood there with my dad on the golf course, that's all I wanted. All I wanted was a relationship with my dad.

No matter what it looks like to the world, God can reconcile my relationships with my kids. It seems impossible to reconcile a healthy and happy relationship with my children, but I know all things are possible with God. They have a right to ask the question, "Where were you for fifteen years? Where were you when I needed to buy school supplies? Where were you to take me to dinner or show up for a baseball game?" And all I can answer is, "I was high and drunk. I took all your money and blew it on drugs, alcohol, gambling, and women."

As my life began to change, I never reached out to my kids because of fear of rejection. I know there's a very strong possibility that there will be a lot of hurtful words. I know that there's a good chance there will be some hatred and there will be some unforgiveness and resentment. While there is no place for excuses, and this is not meant to be one, I know I wouldn't have stayed sober had we started a relationship, and then they told me they couldn't do this. I know that. I know that early on in my sobriety, I couldn't deal with the rejection. Early on in my sobriety, had something happened to my mom or Amy, I wouldn't have been able to stay sober because I wasn't foundationally in place to handle it at that point. If one of my kids said they didn't want anything to do with me and terminated our relationship after starting to build it, I wasn't stable enough to handle the pain, so I would have disappointed my kids all over again. I also allowed Satan to convince me for so long that there was no fixing the relationships. There was no coming back from what I did. There was no hope.

But God showed me nothing is ever too far gone. How do I know? Because God modeled forgiveness. He not only forgave me for my actions and decisions, but also my words. I remember being high on drugs, and my mom picked me up and let me come to her house in Muskogee. I told her that the Bible didn't exist anymore and that it wasn't relevant. I said statements about God and his Word that should have had me condemned for life.

But God forgave me.

A relationship with me does not make sense. I understand from a human perspective that it seems impossible, but I also understand that a guy with a home repair fraud felony should not be running a successful contractor business either. God transformed me so that I can look at my kids and say, "I am a different person. I am a person that you can be proud of, and hopefully, one day, you can call me Dad." God brought men into my life who are strong and led by God to keep me accountable and willing to call me out even before I take a wrong step. I know I can have a positive, healthy, happy relationship and get to know my kids and future grandkids. I'm looking forward to reconciliation and restoration and building back what I destroyed. It's hope. I trust that God will open their hearts, and one day, they will forgive me.

7

UNDESERVED FAVOR

In January of 2015, I made $11 an hour. Over the past eight years, there have been ten days in the history of Living Water that made more money in one day than I made in the entire year of 2015. In 2025, I bought a brand new truck with no money down. I just signed my name and said thank you very much. The salesman at the dealership called me to gather my information. He texted me five minutes later asking what options I wanted and told me he would have it ready for me. I texted back, "Great! I'll pick it up tomorrow morning." In 11 minutes, I bought a truck. During the transaction, the young man saw my income and the company's assets and proceeded to ask me, "What do you think got you to where you are now?" I got to tell him. "Jesus Christ, Amy Wilson, a bunch of discipline and hard work."

When Amy and I met in 2014, I didn't own a vehicle. I lived in a sober community, making $400 a week. I bought a wrecked Dodge Dakota truck from Car Country. It's the only vehicle they would sell me because my credit was so bad. I paid them an exorbitant amount of money. When I questioned the sales guy about the amount, he told me, "If you have other car options you can buy, go buy them." I didn't. So, every two weeks, I had to pay them a crazy amount of money. They overcharged me for the truck, but I paid it anyway. Now, this last truck purchase makes the company's twentieth vehicle.

The Furthest Distance Between Two Points

When Covid hit in 2020, we were not only affected by people being sick, but our supply chain froze. The politicians were talking about bringing out the National Guard and locking everybody in their houses. On March 19, 2020, Amy and I sat at our kitchen table waiting to hear back from the Home Builders Association if we were considered an essential or nonessential business. That meant we would either be allowed to keep running our business or we had to stop working. I was concerned. Amy and I were looking at all our finances, what we had in the bank, what we had coming in, what we could do on credit cards, and what kind of credit lines we could get. I broke down to Amy. Crying, I asked her, "What do I do if they won't let me go to work? We have worked so hard over the past three years to build this business, to employ all these people, and to take care of all these things. What do I do if they won't let me go to work?" Then, I thought back to that day in 2017 when I was crying in the parking lot of Davis Supply Company. That was a catalyst moment in my life. Sitting at my kitchen table, God reminded me that with his help, we would keep going. But this time, it was going to look different.

I've worked very hard. I've put in a ton of hours and a ton of time and a ton of commitment and perseverance and had painful moments. I took zero days off work. It was me with a shovel in a van. But what I realized is that Living Water took priority over everything in my life for about two to three years. The truth is, whenever I heard from God sitting in my car outside the supply house in 2017 to 2019, Living Water was more important than everything. Amy took a backseat to the business every day, as did everybody else including God. But I know God saw the beginning to the end. I figured he thought, "This son is going to get it together. I just need to let him walk this out, and he'll figure out what he needs to do." God blessed my efforts and gave me ridiculous favor, but I did it in my strength. I wasn't relying on him. He was propping me up through his amazing grace, but I wasn't in a position where I relied completely on God. I believe that my heart must have been in the right place. God knew we would be sitting here today. My focus wasn't on the worldly stuff. I didn't really want the money. I just wanted to build the business so I could use the money to give to people who needed it. So, sitting at our kitchen table, Amy and I decided that with God's help, we were going to do anything and everything we could to keep moving forward. We were going to act. We went to work the following day, and something interesting happened. Because a lot of people were forced to stay home and had extra money they weren't spending on vacations and additional expenditures, home improvements moved to the top of people's priority lists. 2020 ended up being a record year for us. Revenue was up over 60% and continued trending that way through 2021. God is so good.

After that, every moment I wasn't working, I was studying, learning, praying, spending time with God, and spending time with people while constantly working on personal development. I now have 38 employees who run my multiple businesses. I get to come in the morning, high-five my employees, inspire and motivate them, and do a slight rudder adjustment when necessary. I pledged to Amy that I would take her on a vacation one week out of the month for the year. I live an amazing life, but I don't deserve it, and I haven't earned it.

The young lady who cuts my hair is a good friend of mine. We coach her business now, and it's an amazing relationship. As she was cutting my hair, we were talking about a trip that Amy and

The Furthest Distance Between Two Points

I were going to take, and she said, "You deserve it." And I said, "No, I don't." She responded, "No, you've earned it." I said, "No, no, I haven't." She asked, "What do you mean? Is this back to your imposter syndrome and your unworthiness?" She was referring to this feeling I have that I've been promoted beyond my abilities and that I don't belong in the position God gave me. I said, "No, no. Not that at all. Not poor self-esteem. Not any of those things whatsoever. Yes, I've absolutely, positively worked very hard for it, but all I deserve is to die in a fiery pit of hell. All I've earned is sin and destruction. All I've done is destroy relationships and destroy people and not be a good father. That's what I deserve and what I earned."

Everything I have and who I am comes from God's unmerited favor and grace. I've done so many wrong things. I'm not just talking about the sin in my life, but what I've done against the law and against people. If I got what I deserved, I should be locked up in prison forever or dead. I've caused a lot of hurt to people, and I've destroyed a lot of relationships. God's grace has covered all my sins, all my destruction, and all the things that I caused. His grace has given me the unmerited favor to step into the fruition of what He's called me to do. I don't deserve any of this. I haven't earned a single bit of it. It's all His. God's grace is sufficient for me because God's power is made perfect in my weakness. In my strength, I was a drug addict, a liar, a manipulator, and a womanizer. That's what I was. But by God's grace, I am not that person anymore. Grace gives you the power to change the condition of your heart, transforming who you once were into who you can become. God's grace means you're never ever too far gone.

People ask me about that all the time about my life and I

struggle to put into words what God has done for me. The nice trucks I own, the pretty house, and the country club membership don't cover up the fact that I was a homeless drug addict. My life is truly a miracle. The Bible is full of stories of remarkable miracles that Jesus performed. He fed 5,000 people with five small loaves of bread and two fish and 4,000 people with seven loaves and a few small fish. He healed multiple people and raised his best friend from the dead. It seems like these stories are in the past since they happened over 2000 years ago, but Jesus is still performing miracles today. And I get to walk out a life full of miracles.

My God-given Strengths

I'm not special. Everyone has the same opportunity as me. I often struggle with, "God, why do you allow me to have all this?" For a long time, I didn't feel worthy enough to wear the watch I wear now and go play a ridiculously expensive round of golf. I recently went on a road trip to visit a customer with multiple locations across the country. As I was driving and thinking through my story and how I didn't deserve what he's given me, God told me it was because he knew I'd give away the money. He said, "There's no way you will ever feel you earned that. So just give it away." So, I believe that's why he did it for me. He said, "I know what you're going to do with what I've given you. You'll have some nice things, and you'll spend money on some stupid stuff, but you're also going to pay that guy's house payment, and you'll pay for that lady to get her transmission fixed, and you'll buy that person who needs a vehicle a truck." It's what I saw my grandpa do his entire life. He made good money driving a truck, but he was broke the day he died because he gave everything away to help people. He grew up with nothing. He lived through the Great Depression. I remember sitting at the kitchen table and him telling me a story. "My daddy told me I had to leave the house at 12 years old because he couldn't feed me. It wasn't because he hated me or anything else, but he had to feed my sisters. So, he said good luck, and I left. I had nothing, so having anything is amazing." That's how I live.

One of my gifts is giving. God knew he could take my unworthiness and show me how worthy I am—that I'm his child. He did a complete reversal of how I viewed money. Money isn't for my benefit. Money is given to us by God to steward well. It's all his, anyway.

I look back at my life, and I can see how I used the gifts God gave me for my benefit. I perverted them. I was gifted with the ability to work hard and do things that many people, day in and day out, can't do consistently. Years ago, I was making money to go get high and drunk. Now, when I use my money for God, I make an abundance and an overflow of cash that I can pour into where God wants me to use it. The perverted version of my gifts never had the tenfold yield that the God version does. When you take my work ethic and align it with the will of God, the result is exponential. Hard work alone brings about amazing wealth and amazing results, but when that hard work is applied with God's principles, it produces ten times what it would have. There is a much greater return on your investment.

Previously, my ability to speak Spanish connected me to Mexicans and Colombians to buy cocaine for a cheap price. Now, I use Spanish to speak to my employees, allowing me to have a team of Caucasian, Mexican, and Hispanic descendants from Guatemala, Honduras, and Puerto Rico that can all work with me to build what God intends for us to build. Often, my mornings consist of me flipping back and forth between speaking Spanish to some employees and English to others about installs, sales, and schedules.

When I used my words to semantically crush people, I manipulated them and made them feel less than. After I beat them down, I made them reliant on my words of affirmation. I previously used my sales skills and my ability to steer a conversation to get what I wanted. I understood at a young age that if you use someone's name, make eye contact, make sure your body language is inviting, understand other people's body language, and don't ever ask yes or no questions, you can lead people in the direction you want them to go. I would tell four different people four different stories, and they would all be in the same room, but I would spin the story to benefit myself to whoever was listening. I actually enjoyed the fact that they were all in the same room and couldn't figure out that I was a pathological liar.

Now, I use my words for positivity, encouragement, development, and growth. When put to work for God, those same exact skills produce abundant results, including three back-to-back record months for Living Water. We did more sales in the month of March than we ever have. April beat March, and May beat April. God showed me that when we are obedient, he produces a harvest. After years of sowing seeds, we are seeing the fruits of our labor. I make ten times the money I made before, and I lead employees in several companies I own with the same set of skills I had before but the difference is that those skills are no longer being perverted. Instead, they are being used for God.

The Furthest Distance Between Two Points

I never could figure out what this fire was inside me that got me up so early in the morning and allowed me to wake up every single day with super high energy and great enthusiasm. I never got tired. It started when I was a little kid. I realized it's my severe attention-deficit/hyperactivity disorder (ADHD) that I was diagnosed with at a young age. I was off the charts with ADHD. Because of my disorder, my life growing up was never consistent. I couldn't stick to anything. I jumped from here to there, girl to girl, and house to house. I couldn't focus on anything, but I could process information quickly. I could process the entire conversation before a person even finished a sentence. I was fifty sentences ahead of a person in a conversation, so I steered the whole discussion to my advantage.

People would shut down and stop talking. Now, my ability to keep going without my energy draining works towards God's benefit of building what he needs me to build without burnout. I can process the next fifteen steps necessary to build the business or move us to the next level because I can see the result. I can see the entire process from beginning to end and know how to get there. I can also remember details and retain information at a ridiculous rate. That's why I'm so good at sales. I can remember people's names, faces, objections, and even their favorite things. Those skills allowed me to manipulate people in the past. Now, I'm able to use my gifts as a strength.

There's a story about a boy named Joseph who was sold into slavery by his brothers. He was later accused and thrown in jail for something he didn't do. Although he appears to be forgotten about, years later, he winds up becoming second in command to lead the country of Egypt, and he saves the Egyptians and his entire family from starving to death due to a drought. As he reflects on his life and the trials and difficulties he went through, he recognizes that his path led him to save tens of thousands of lives. Years later, as he faces his brothers with tears, he tells them that what they intended for harm, God intended for good to save many lives. My ADHD was what the enemy used to harm me and spin me out of control. Severe ADHD is now an asset of mine instead of a liability.

What I know now at 47 years old is that who I am now is exactly who God created me to be to fulfill the exact purpose for which I'm cuurrently walking out. All of what I thought were deficiencies or weaknesses in me and all the parts of me that I thought were negatives are actually strengths that are building my testimony for God's glory.

8

GOD'S INTENTIONALITY

If I tell people I have a home repair fraud felony, an embezzlement felony, and that I got kicked out of the Air Force because I helped a girl spend a bunch of money, they will probably decide they need another sprinkler guy. They will find someone else to do the job because they would not trust me or trust me with their kids. That is what makes this part of my story so incredible. Standing in a new client's garage, I told her I was a former drug addict and had previously made bad decisions. I had no idea this meeting would affect the rest of my life and the trajectory of so many others.

The events took place in the spring of 2020. I did an estimate on this woman's sprinkler system. She wanted a standard sprinkler system, but her daughter wanted to put in a garden zone so the sprinklers would automatically water the garden area that her daughter planned to build with her grandfather. I talked through all the details and put the bid together.

A week later, I followed up like I always do. During the conversation, the woman said to me, "I'm going to go with you, Josh. I'm going to have you install our sprinklers even though you're $1,500 more expensive than the other two bids I received." I said, "Well, I really appreciate that." She said, "I know I'm supposed to go with you. It's what God told me to do." I said, "Well, ma'am, thank you, and I appreciate the obedience. I think it's really neat that you're willing to do that." I didn't really think of the impact of it at that time.

Six weeks later, we came to do her sprinkler installation. After the install, I stopped in her garage to do a quick demo like we do for every new client, and we started talking. She shared with me that she knew before she even met me that she was supposed to hire me. She told me that in her quiet time with God, God kept taking her to the phrase "Living Water," and those words were all over her journal. She knew immediately after googling sprinkler installation companies that Living Water Irrigation was who God had chosen. As a single mom, she shared with me that she and her kids had been through a lot in their lives. She told me her husband passed away seven and a half years ago when her kids were 8 and 10 years old. That's when I shared with her that I made a bunch of poor decisions. I made my life rough. She asked me what I meant.

It was then, standing in her garage, that I told my story to a stranger for the first time.

I kept thinking, "I cannot believe I am telling this lady my story." I told her that I made a bunch of bad decisions with drugs and alcohol. I told her I was a terrible person, that I do not have a relationship with my kids, and I was a former drug addict.

She asked me what verse in the Bible inspired the company name, "Living Water." I told her, "John 7:38. 'Whoever believes in me, as Scripture has said, rivers of living water will flow from within them.'"

She asked me, "Why John 7:38? Why did you choose 'Living Water?'"

I shared with her that Amy and I were in church one Sunday when our pastor, Pastor Jim Carney at Current Church, preached a message on John 7:38. After church, we were on our way to lunch, and my mom called me. She said, "I have a name for the business." She told me her pastor at World Outreach Church preached on John 7:38. And I said, "Well, Mom, my pastor preached on John 7:38 too, so we're going to name it Living Water Irrigation." I said, "I've already looked it up." At the time, there were three Living Water Irrigation Companies in the country. But we knew that was the name.

I told the young woman that I had been so fortunate to be able to build this business. She told me her son, who was going to be a junior in high school, was interested in business and entrepreneurship and was looking to go to business school after he graduated college. And I said, "Well, he can come hang out with me if he wants. Tell him to be at my office on Tuesday at 5:00 am."

The next day, I received a text from her son. "Mr. Wilson, this is Maximus. My mom told me about the opportunity on Tuesday. I will be there at 5:00 am. Is this the correct address? 12308 E 60th St, Tulsa, OK 74146, United States. Thank you for this opportunity. I look forward to meeting you."

I texted back. "Absolutely, buddy. I'm looking forward to meeting you."

He replied, "I'm looking forward to meeting you also."

Three days later, I confirmed the time. "Hey, buddy. Tomorrow at 5:30 am. I will not be at the office until then."

On Tuesday, June 30, 2020, at 5:30 am, a seventeen-year-old boy I had never before met walked into my office.

A Selfless Decision

Prior to that day, I never stopped for anything. I get in my own way so many times. I had done over a thousand demos of sprinkler systems before I went to this young woman's house, and they always went like this: "Here's how the controller works. This is how you turn it on and off. Here's how you program it. Your sprinklers work great. You have my cell number. If you ever need to reach me, we'll honor a warranty. Thank you very much." I make some simple adjustments and leave. Normally, I pick up the check, do a demo, and leave.

But I stopped. I know what stopped me in the garage that day. It was God himself who stopped me because I never would have stopped on my own. When I told my close friend and mentor what happened, he asked me how the conversation got so deep. I told him it was the first time I stopped. Because I'm always going.

So here was this boy in my office, eagerly waiting to learn from me. Every Tuesday that summer of 2020, Maximus showed up at 5:30 am. I always had meetings on Tuesdays. We met with my business coach, and then I would record a podcast. I set up lunches with successful business owners so he could ask questions and get to know them.

As time passed, our relationship got closer and closer. I was so amazed at the positive choices that Maximus made after his father died, even with that level of pain and heartache, because I hadn't chosen to make the positive choices and go the positive route. I chose the opposite path.

Through his senior year, we continued to talk and spend time together. Maximus graduated valedictorian of his high school. I was so fortunate to sit in his graduation as he gave his valedictorian speech. He spoke about what God did in his life. Then he mentioned me and the influence I had on his life. It was a humbling moment.

Our seven-year relationship turned from a mentorship to a friendship to a deep connection that I can only imagine is what it is like to have a relationship with a son. I get to watch him grow and make life decisions. We navigate life together even though he goes to school out of state and has spent the last two summers interning in different states. Every Sunday, we talk. He asks for my advice, and I get to tell him what I think. And he listens.

I always knew God drew us together for a reason, but not until I started writing this book did I realize the depth of what God was doing through his divine plan. Mentoring Maximus was the first time I made an intentional decision to be unselfish. I wanted nothing out of the relationship. We all make decisions with a motive, whether it is positive or negative. Most of my relationships were always me either selling to people or closing sales for the business. There was always an agenda. When Maximus walked through my door that Tuesday morning at 5:30 am, I made a decision—I'm not going to fail this kid.

I had one of two choices. I could let him hang out, meet a couple people, and send him on his way. "Hey buddy, have a good one. Wish you nothing but the best. See you when I see you" or I can do what we've done now. Early on in my relationship with Maximus, my mentor asked me if I was prepared to have this kid in my life forever. I told him yes, I was. I knew what my yes meant. I was making the commitment to pour into his life with no expectations of anything in return. It wasn't about sex or drugs or money or success or accomplishment or fame or clout or ego or anything. It was about a young man who had a desire to be better and just wanted my two cents worth of wisdom. Expectations cause strain, stress, and strife. Expectations cause disappointment, resentment, and anger. I never expected anything of Maximus. I just wanted to help him.

Jesus would call it serving. That's what we are told to do. That's what Jesus did. He served people. That's all Jesus ever did. His entire ministry, his entire walk, all he did was serve. If we want to be Christlike, we have to serve others instead of being served. Jesus' ultimate service to humanity was when he gave up his life for ours.

Even though I chose to serve Maximus, I didn't realize the magnitude of that choice until I was driving through the hills of North Carolina on my way to Tennessee. God revealed to me that I could care about somebody else more than I cared about my own selfish desires and more than I cared about myself. I haven't been a father to my two boys or my daughter. I haven't been in their lives. I failed. There's no other way to put it. I flat out failed. But God showed me that I could be unselfish. And it had to be a stranger. There had to be no attachment, bias, or family connection to the person. It had to be someone around the age of my own children. God knew it had to be a goofy kid who works out too much to teach me how to be selfless instead of selfish.

Prior to meeting Maximus, there's no way that I would have helped coach people through recovery. There's no way I would have stepped away from my evening of watching sports or hanging out with my wife to stay on the phone with a guy who wants to get high or step off the golf course because somebody's struggling with their business. Even though I was living my life for Christ and was a good husband and a good person, I wasn't selfless. My willingness to serve others and be on the phone for long periods of time to talk through people's problems and addictions or help coach them through business questions began with Maximus.

The rest of my life isn't about me anymore. It's about God and his glory and about what I can do to make an impact for God in other people's lives. Yes, I get to do a lot of cool stuff for myself. But the revelation in my truck that day led me to see my purpose, that this business that we've built and this financial success that we've had has allowed me to reach out to help others. It's like the ripple effect when you drop a rock in the lake or the butterfly effect, which is the idea that when a small butterfly flaps its wings, the effect eventually creates a typhoon. In just the short period of time that I've chosen to live my life for Jesus, we have been able to affect numerous lives and positively influence others by sim-ply choosing to serve instead of being served. I'm living out what God's purpose is for my life, and it all started in my office on a Tuesday morning at 5:30 am when I made a decision that I was going to give that young man everything I had.

Maximus is not only one of the most important people in my life, but he has also changed my life. That's how serious and intentional God is. He brought this young man into my life to make me a better person. I learned that a real relationship with real love and Christ-like behavior means no expectations. We serve others out of love. God is shaping me and making me a better person by putting people in my path to mold and refine me. God is the potter. We are clay. God reworks us, forming us into the shape that is the best version of ourselves. Maximus challenges me every single day to be the best version of me. And God challenges me to make sure that I am available and giving Maximus the best I have. My hope is that one day, my children will get to see my best.

Until I started living a life for Jesus, I never realized how intentional God really is. God is in every detail of our lives. Months after meeting Maximus, I found out that he was born on October 19th. He shares the exact same birthday as my oldest son.

Nothing is accidental or coincidental.

And God doesn't make mistakes. We do.

Choosing Right or Wrong

One of the reasons Maximus and I have such a close relationship is because our lives are parallel. In many ways, we are the exact same person. If you look at where we're at in terms of athleticism, our ability to communicate, or our intelligence, we're almost identical. Where we differ is my life took this horrible detour while he remained on a straight path.

Maximus last saw his dad when he was 10 years old. He chose to turn to Jesus.

The last time I saw my dad before trying to reconcile at the golf course was Christmas when I was 10. I chose to turn to women, sex, drugs, and alcohol.

Maximus is now 21 and about to graduate from Texas A&M University. He chose to go to college and is on his way to law school.

At 21 years old, I chose to sleep with a young lady that I just met and had a baby.

We differ because Maximus makes better choices.

If you ask Maximus and me who one of the most influential persons in our life is, we will tell you, our grandfathers. Both men stepped in and took the role of our fathers. They both gave wise advice. The majority of what I know about business came from my grandfather, even though he only had a third-grade education. The most valuable things I own are my grandfather's kitchen table and his chair. The table I spent years of my life sitting at is upstairs in my house, and his chair sits in my office. I remember talking with my grandfather at that table when I was 20 years old, and him telling me not to go to Vegas. I remember the conversation like it was yesterday. Maximus takes every piece of advice he is given by his grandfather and walks out what his grandfather tells him. He chooses to listen. I chose not to. I took the advice my grandfather gave me and did the exact opposite. I ruined the opportunity to listen to the one man I should have trusted most because I chose to feed my selfish desires.

Two Parallel Lives, Two Different Choices

I made two destructive choices that altered the trajectory of my life, and everything else was a direct result of those two decisions. However, my poor decision-making started when I was young. I was the youngest child, and because I've always been gregarious and able to speak with charm and enthusiasm, my choices were never scrutinized, and my decisions were never forced to be right. I stole some Jolly Ranchers when I was 6 years old. You hear stories of how a kid has to go back to the store and mop the floors and right the wrong, but that didn't happen to me. I never got caught.

A few weeks later, my middle brother stole from the store. My mom found out, and he had to go back and tell them what he had done. I kept getting away with stuff. I never had consequences for blaming my brothers and saying they did it, or choosing not to do my homework because I could ace the tests, or talking in school and getting away with it because I was funny, or cheating on the playground at tetherball. The lack of consequences led me to con-tinue making poor decisions, just on a much bigger scale. I loved being able to get away with something. It's called gaslighting.

Gaslighting is the ability to convince somebody of something by forcing them to question what they know. It's a way to gain power and control over another person. I could go through hundreds of scenarios and examples where I convinced someone of something. I loved lying to people. I loved manipulating people. What I didn't realize at the time was that there really were consequences. My choices hurt countless numbers of people. I didn't consider how the decisions I made then would affect my future and the future of those around me. As a 20-year-old hormonal kid, the last thing on my mind on New Year's Eve was getting pregnant. My brain didn't even compute that as an option. I was more concerned about my self-gratification than my choices. I didn't consider the thought, "What does this do to my life if I choose to do this?" nor did I consider, "What does this do to another person's life if I choose to do this?" I did not think about how my choices would change the trajectory of someone else's life. If you look at my son's mother's life and her choices, she took full advantage of what the military can offer. At 37 years old, she retired with two master's degrees. She also chose to raise our son, who is a great man from what I know of him. She made positive choices. She's a great mom. I hate what I did to her. It wasn't right. My choices hurt them and all those people around me when all they wanted was what was best for me.

That's all my grandfather ever wanted. He wanted what was best for me because he loved me.

My grandfather wanted what my heavenly father wanted: for me to be the man God created me to be, to be a loving husband and father, to pour back into the community, to give and care for others, and to serve others. Neither one of them wanted me to hurt. Neither of them wanted me to go through the twenty years that I chose. They didn't want me to go through all the pain. God just wanted to give me good gifts and a good life. He wants that for all of us. God has so much more for us, but often, we aren't willing to accept what he wants. We are so caught up in what we want that we don't even recognize that he has something better for us.

The Furthest Distance Between Two Points

We can't go to God with a closed fist because if we do, we can't receive anything God tries to give us. When I chose to quit running from God, he poured out his wisdom, guidance, and direction with love, care, and compassion that is far beyond what our earthly fathers can provide. I filter my choices through God's Word and constantly go to Him for answers because He always makes perfect decisions.

Like Maximus, I now make positive choices. I have several men and women in my life that I can go to for counsel. I'm willing to accept correction and change direction when I am heading down the wrong path. Because I seek Godly wisdom from others and choose to listen, I skip a lot of pain and hurt.

God's intentionality of how and why He brought Maximus and I together demonstrates how detailed God is in His plans to grow us into who He wants us to become. God has a plan and can and will do amazing things if we are willing to be obedient and listen to Him. The remarkable part of this story is that the entire course of my life and Maximus' life was affected by one mother's choice to obey God. One woman's choice to make a decision that didn't make any financial sense changed the rest of our lives. She chose to say yes to God. Maximus chose to say yes to the opportunity. And I chose to finally say yes to laying down my selfish desires. Those yeses changed the trajectory of all our lives.

I used to look at my relationship with Maximus and wonder why he listens to me. I believe it's because of trust and credibility. He trusts me. He trusts that I will give him answers that God guides me to give him. I had men and women in my life that I chose not to listen to. I'm sure you have people in your life who have been there for you, those men and women who love you enough to tell you the truth, even when you don't want to hear it. If you think of all the advice you've received from them and consider why you chose not to listen, you will begin to learn something about yourself, and you might even realize they were right.

9

THE FURTHEST DISTANCE BETWEEN TWO POINTS

Highway 169 is one of the main highways in the Tulsa area and is the road that leads to my house in Owasso, Oklahoma. I drive it every day, south to north and north to south. Whenever traffic backs up, there is one area that always gets congested. A lot of trucks, including myself, bypass the traffic by going down the embankment. One day, on my drive home, I noticed the city put caution signs and cones blocking the self-made dirt ramp. Highway patrol sits there now. I don't take the shortcut anymore.

Just like the embankment on Highway 169, I made my own path in life by diverting from what God intended for me. I jumped off the road. I drove through the ditches. I didn't care about the consequences. God clearly defined a path for me. God never promises our life will be free from pain. My dad left. There are going to be struggles and heartaches. God tells us we will have troubles in this world.

But God already knows that. He sees what is going to happen in our lives and knows the best path for us. All God wanted me to do was drive from South Jenks to North Owasso. That's all he wanted me to do: drive from north to south on Highway 169 of life. But I chose to take all these off-road extravaganzas. I chose to get off the path he intended for me and opted for the shortcuts that led me to the ditches. I could have reached a completely different point in my life in a much shorter way. The path God intended me to travel was easier, more direct, and less destructive. He wanted me to take the right path. God tried to prevent me from taking the longer one. I could have chosen not to make my own short-cuts. Instead, I went off-roading in the mud and muck. Shortcuts are messy. We find ourselves lost, in a ditch, or at a dead-end, and much like my truck when I took the shortcut, I got dirty. I took the longest path to reach the point where God wanted me to be.

The furthest distance between two points is the sin that separates us from the cross. Sin creates a chasm preventing us from entering a closeness and communion with Christ. Ultimately, our life is based on one decision. Do we choose sin, or do we choose Christ? This was always my choice. I was separated from Christ by my own decision. I chose the longest path. There was never an exit God intended me to take. I just went off-roading on a series of winding paths of sin.

We make choices that are the furthest or the closest distance to the cross. The further away we are, the darker it is. The closer we are to the cross, the lighter it is because Jesus is light. Not only is He light of the dark world, but anyone who follows Him will never walk in darkness. I made decisions in darkness. I was so far away from Jesus. God was there every single time with a better option. He was there when my dad left. He saw my need and tried to fill it. "Josh, I am going to give you all these great men in your life." When I did cocaine for the first time, God tried again. "We need to go get you on medicine to regulate your ADHD." I chose not to. When my heart was broken the first time, he brought me someone else. He kept trying to give me other options.

God tells us he has a way out for us. He tells us that no one is tempted beyond what we can bear and that He will provide a way out of the temptation. God kept trying to steer me back on the road, and I chose to take different routes instead. God's option was not the fun thing to do. It did not satisfy my selfish needs.

Every time you sin, every time you make a bad choice, a subtraction occurs from God's intention for your life. When a positive deposit happens, you add to your life. You can look at it from a business perspective. Subtraction always removes and lessens the end result. Addition always adds value. It's a compounding effect. The more that is added, the greater the outcome. The greater the outcome, the more that is added.

I was 25 years old when I worked for a major Asian chain restaurant. When the company decided to open the restaurants in the Tennessee market, my boss planned to move to Tennessee, which is why they were going to leave me all six Oklahoma stores to run. At the current revenue and operating rate, I would have made between $250-$300,000 a year with bonuses at 27 years old. If you look at that trajectory of that path and consider that I would probably be an operating partner and then a development partner, I would have been making half a million dollars a year in my early thirties. I would have become an entrepreneur earlier, making more than I make today. If I had chosen to stay on the expressway God mapped for me, look where I could have been instead.

When I finally chose the straight path, I could hear God saying, "Wash your dirty truck, get back on the road I paved for you, and let's go. You were supposed to be here at 23, but okay, you got here at 35. Let's go." I know what God's Word says is true because

The Furthest Distance Between Two Points

I've lived it. God took what Satan intended for evil and turned it into good. Through the restoration and reconciliation power of God, I'm back to exactly where I was supposed to be, but at age 47. No more off-roading for me. There's no more subtraction, only addition.

Every choice I made to detour, God has flipped to the complete opposite. That's why I'm so far away from who I used to be. I used to live a detached life. Now, I have deep relationships with people. I used to make selfish decisions. Now, I strive to be selfless. I used to be insecure. Now, I am confident. I'm learning, too. Had I not been such a horrible father, I would not recognize what it means to be a good father. Not only am I the opposite of what I was, I make decisions opposite of the sins I chose in my past. My story is about the transformation that had to occur so I could get on the right path to get to today. The right path is God's path.

The gentleman who taught me how to fix sprinklers is the best sprinkler tech I've ever met. To this day, he's better at fixing sprinklers than me. When I met him, I was at the point where I decided to change my life. My life got better. However, his got worse. I found out a few years later that he was in jail. We made different choices. We reversed directions. He went down the path that I left. I chose to move forward towards a hopeful future. I chose to follow Jesus.

I look at the difference between my choices and Maximus' decisions. There are a million similarities between me and him, but when we look at my choices versus his and the paths we chose to take, there are zero similarities. There is a song by Mercy Me called "Dear Younger Me." What would I tell my younger self? I consider myself a good man now. But I would've been a great man had I chosen what God intended for me and skipped all the heartache. My definition of "great" isn't what the world typically defines it as because the world defines success as money. A young man once commented to me, "I want to be successful in life." I replied, "What's successful, buddy? Do you view me as successful?" He said, "Yes. Tremendously." I responded, "I haven't seen my kids in sixteen years." I've missed a lot of the greater things in my life.

I never realized how important my decisions were at 16 and 17 years old. The obvious detour was the first time I did cocaine, but if you look back at the path of my life, losing my virginity is where the breakdown started. I lost my purity. I broke the commitment I made to myself and to God that I would wait until I got married to have sex. After losing my virginity, I opened the door to following other destructive paths. Sinful choices became easier decisions. The voice inside me stopped differentiating between right and wrong.

Sin doesn't start as sin. Sin is first conceived in the mind before the action takes place. It starts as a seed, and as it's fed more thoughts, it grows and turns into action, which becomes the sin. My thoughts with my first girlfriend were, "We are going to get married. We are in love. We are going to live happily ever after," so I justified the action in my brain. I opened the door for the next thought, "Relationships aren't that important. It's not about love and connection and covenant and how God designed sexual relations. It's about my desires." So, I had sex again with my next girlfriend. Since I had sex, smoking didn't seem like a big deal. My smoking addiction shortened the road to other drugs. Nicotine's a drug, right? What's the difference with a little cocaine? The willingness to do drugs and

The Furthest Distance Between Two Points

the unwillingness to choose Christ started way before the two lines of cocaine.

The furthest distance between two points included the choices I made to run away from God and to live my life the way I wanted to live it. It's just like the story of a son in the Bible. The son didn't care about his dad. His actions considered his dad dead because he asked for his inheritance early. He decided he was going to squander everything he had and do it his own way. I did the same thing. I created the separation from my heavenly dad. I created the distance. I jumped on the road to destruction and ran straight to hell. I didn't just detour through a ditch off Highway 169, I dug a trench, and as I kept digging and digging further and further down, it got darker and darker until there was no more light. But the moment I chose to turn back to the cross and said yes to Jesus, the distance closed immediately. Everything got bright.

I owe God my life. If it weren't for God's sacrificial love sending His only son from heaven to earth to die for all of us, and if Christ wasn't willing to give up His life on the cross for me, I would still be living in a dark pit. There is a king in the Bible named David who understands being in a helpless pit of destruction. When he was sinking into a slimy pit, he knew that he could not rescue himself. So, he turned to God.

Psalm 40:1-3 is one of the most amazing passages in the Bible.

> 1 I waited patiently for the Lord;
> he turned to me and heard my cry.

> 2 He lifted me out of the slimy pit,

out of the mud and mire;
he set my feet on a rock
and gave me a firm place to stand.

3 He put a new song in my mouth,
a hymn of praise to our God.
Many will see and fear the Lord
and put their trust in him.

God pulled me from the depths of darkness, but I had to choose to turn to Him for help. The previous story of the son who left home and squandered everything didn't end with his destructive decision. He made a choice. He chose to go home, and when he did, his father came running after him with open arms, love, and forgiveness. I did what the son did. I chose to go home, and like the father in the story, my Heavenly Father came running to me. As soon as I made the choice to turn to the cross, the distance shortened. As soon as I chose Jesus, the gap that once was so far away closed immediately. He was there with open arms, love, and forgiveness. The love of the God our Father is not conditional. God was there all along. "I'm right here, Josh. I've never been far away from you. I've been here the whole time." He tells us He will never leave us or forsake us. My eyes opened to how intentional He was throughout my life, including sending me father figures at a very young age. God tried to give me bumpers and steer me in the right direction by bringing those men into my life. I didn't recognize God was my real Father until I got sober and stopped making wrong choices. I finally understood who God is. I finally understood love. God is love. And God has no expectations except for us to love Him, which is easy because love has no expectations.

The Furthest Distance Between Two Points

The transformation in my life started when I chose Jesus, but it continued with me creating a habit of making the right choices. Instead of compounding negative choices, I compounded positive ones. Our positive choices start in the mind. "I shouldn't have gone to this party. I shouldn't be here. But now that I'm there, I'm going to leave because my habit is to make good choices. I thought we were playing ping pong and eating pizza. I didn't know there would be liquor bottles and people partying. Thanks for the invite. I'm going home." I learned to make different decisions by looking through God's lens, not the world's, and continued to make the right choices. "I don't have to worry about going to jail today." I make another right choice. "I don't have to try to cover up a story with my mom." I make the next right choice. "I can actually pay my bills." I make another right choice. "I don't have to explain to Amy what I've done because I chose not to do it." I make another right choice, "I'm going to remove the negative people from my life and replace them with positive people."

I continue to make the next right choice and do the next right thing. God revealed to me that a continual habit of good choices creates positive results. It's a daily choice. It's a formed habit leading to my own definition of success. Success is the direct result of the overcoming. The overcoming can be anything in life and requires long-term commitment and hard work because there are no shortcuts to success.

Overcoming is like exercising a muscle. When we work out, we destroy our muscles, and as they build back, the muscles are strengthened. The struggle, stress, and strain are what create the increased strength. For my life, I chose the easy path. I was unwilling to face the hurt and the pain of what happened with my dad and mom. The avoidance of the struggle is what created the decades of destruction.

The Real Enemies

Every choice is inherently good or bad. If we choose good, good comes out of it. If we choose bad, bad comes out of it. Either way, we wind up facing an enemy. The world's enemy is Satan, but our individual enemies are the demons we face every day that take over our minds, body, and soul. When I avoided facing my enemies head-on and turned and ran, I gave Satan a way into my life that he used later to desensitize my decision-making.

I opened the door for Satan, and he came right in and took over my home. He will always figure out a way to get into our house. He knew he could get me through money and sex. It wasn't just the act of having sex. It was a complete destruction of my relationship with Christ. The initial breakdown was my lack of confidence because of people making fun of me because of my faith. I wasn't strong enough to stand on solid ground in my beliefs. He used my insecurities and my dad leaving and then sex and money and got a foothold in my life. The root of my sin was selfishness.

Because I turned away from facing my enemies, I could never stop and fight. I ran until I was 36 years old. For twenty years, I took shortcuts to skip the pain. I detoured to avoid the storms. While it's a longer distance to exit Highway 169 when taking the side roads during an Oklahoma thunderstorm, it's much easier to take the side roads to avoid the storms than to drive straight through them. The problem is if you don't go through the storm, you will never learn how to navigate stormy weather. You can't take shortcuts with God.

The Furthest Distance Between Two Points

You just delay your life. When you take the shortcut, you won't learn what you're supposed to when you are supposed to, and you won't be prepared to walk out the blessings and the life God has for you.

Going through the pain was necessary. The struggle had to happen. I had to stand and face the hurts before I could ever overcome them. I had to get to a point where I was healed and whole, and then I gained an understanding that my father was just a hurt little boy like me, and my mom didn't understand how to show love. I had to stand and face my enemy, but I didn't do it alone. Jesus was standing right there with me. The enemy comes to steal, kill, and destroy, but Jesus comes so that we may have life and have it to the fullest. Jesus came to fight my battle with me and for me, and I chose to stand and fight with Him by my side. But the fight was work. Our thoughts can still betray us. It's always easier to go after what the enemy wants and after my own selfish desires. Those don't require any effort. I fought back by blocking thoughts the enemy would try to put in my head by praying. I replaced thoughts that tried to detour me by quoting Scripture. I listened to God's voice, which kept me accountable. I took negative thoughts captive in my mind. If a woman walked by me on the street, I immediately thought of Amy. I made sure that my thoughts were controlled, and by God's power and authority, I conquered each battle.

When we choose the cross, our decisions are led by God's Spirit instead of our own desires. When I look at all the people who have faced adversity and not become a victim of it, they all chose to overcome instead of become their circumstances. I became a drug addict. I became a liar. I became a criminal and a convict. I could have overcome those things instead of becoming those things.

Maximus could have taken a completely different path. But he didn't. And God brought him into my life as part of my strengthening. God showed me how my life would have been different in a positive way. Maximus didn't take the detour. He chose to face the obstacles he needed to overcome. We were on the same path, but I chose a different one. We were like two cars traveling down the same highway, both with the same destination in mind: to serve God and to serve others. While one of those cars kept going towards the destination, the other car started driving crazy. It ended up getting pulled over and didn't get back on track until twenty years later.

Maximus' life is proof of what happens when you make the right choices when you choose Jesus. Because of his choices, I can show other young men how life can go wrong and how life can go right when they are facing trials in their lives. The trials and struggles will come. But the solution is to take it to the cross. We put so much effort into trying to control the outcome, but we can't. We worry and lose sleep and have health problems trying to make situations work with our effort and in our strength. If we create a habit of good choices and run everything through the filter of God's Word, then we stop trying to do it our way and let God do it his way. The popular phrase, "What would Jesus do?" is really a good standard for our lives.

When I look at Maximus, I see myself. It's like looking in a mirror, because what I realized is, when I chose not to fail him, I didn't want to fail me either. And most importantly, I didn't want to fail God. I spent all those years making bad choices. I fell in love with chasing the sin. It's an unpopular conversation to have, but I had a lot of fun. And that's just the truth of it. I enjoyed the fact that

The Furthest Distance Between Two Points

I would have a bunch of money and literally nowhere to sleep. Whether I spent it all on cocaine, lost it at the casino, gambled, or got drunk, I liked the stress and drama of it. It gave me a high. Once I chose Jesus, my life became simple and rewarding.

I realized how the life I led was a false way of living. It was chaos. Satan loves chaos. We invite Satan into our minds and our lives when we sin.

When God ran to me that day, He took the furthest distance between two points—my sin and the cross and turned them into the shortest distance between two points. My Heavenly Father wrapped His arms around me that day. I coach people now who struggle with the same destructive decisions and habits that I did. I tell them to write down all their destructive choices and behaviors and then do the complete opposite of everything they used to do. That is how we create positive living.

10

REWRITING THE LIES

Satan uses lies as a trap to prevent us from walking in what God purposed us to do on this earth. I went from believing "I'm not worthy to sit with these people at this golf course" to "I'm on a boat with a billionaire watching whales." I had to overcome the lie that I wasn't good enough.

Many of us believe lies, and we don't realize we believe them. "I don't belong here." "I'm not worthy enough." "I'm going to fail." These lies run through our heads and affect our decisions and choices. God created us for a reason and gave us specific gifts and talents to impact others' lives. If Satan can get us to believe the lies, we remain in prison. He locks us up, and we are unable to do what God created us for and prepared in advance for us to do.

Satan convinced me my identity was a drug addict. My mom didn't think I was good enough, and my dad left me because I was not worthy enough for him to stay. I had to learn how to take the lies I believed and rewrite them into truths. It's the power of manifestation. Manifestation is taking an idea, an event, or an object and turning it into something. Manifestation requires action. We must rewrite the lie from where we are to where we want to be. If you think you belong in the room, you belong in the room. If you think you are a great salesperson, you're a great salesperson. If you think you're a great father, you will be a great father.

We are what we think about, and we become what we focus on, either good or bad. If I think I'm a terrible father, a horrible husband, a cheater, a liar, an alcoholic, and a drug addict, that's what I'll always be. The turning point for me was in Celebrate Recovery when I recognized that whatever I think about will manifest in my life. If I think I'm sick, I will be sick. If I think I'm tired, I'm going to be tired. If I think I'm miserable, I'm going to be miserable. I can speak life over myself, or I can speak death. We speak what is in our hearts, and whatever I speak over myself is what my heart believes.

There are some interesting studies of psychiatrists and psychologists who researched serial killers and sex addicts. They became what they studied. If you spend time obsessing over a subject, you become it. I obsess over making sure I only think about positive and optimistic things in my life. I use my obsession to create positivity in my daily activities. I frame my world in a way that I'm going to win. I always focus on what is and can go right.

"Whatever we plant in our subconscious mind and nourish with repetition and emotion will one day become a reality." – Earl Nightingale.

Our reality becomes our truth. But as Earl Nightingale states, the reality happens one day with nourishment and repetition. The process takes time. When a bamboo tree is planted, it takes five years of meticulous watering and care before it breaks through the ground. Even though you see nothing, the plant requires daily watering and maintenance. After five years, the tree shoots up and can grow to 90 feet tall in five weeks.

The problem is that today's society wants immediate gratification, which is the opposite of working hard and persevering. Investing in ourselves or anything we want for that length of time is challenging. My 4:00 am wake-up call happened every single day for five years. After five years, our investment grew to 90 feet tall, and it's continuing to grow. Living Water Irrigation is exponentially more than I could ever have dreamed of or hoped for. I'm excited to see where the company is five weeks and five years from now. It's exactly what God tells us. God is able to do immeasurably more than all we ask or imagine, according to his power that is at work within us.

You have to profess who you are. I'm a sober person. I'm a great husband. I'm a great businessman. I'm a great leader. I'm a great manager. I'm a great salesman. It's not arrogant. It is the belief in whom God made you to be. Even if your circumstances or your current position don't show it. Then someday, in five weeks, or five years, or whenever God's perfect timing is, it will manifest. Every successful person you've ever talked to, every great father, every great pastor, every great business owner, and every great husband spent years investing without expecting an immediate return. Google the name "Jeff Bezos." In 1996, he was in a garage. Now, you know him as the founder of Amazon, one of the most valuable companies in the world. Apple computers also started in a garage. We don't always see the fruition of what we've invested in for years. We must take incremental steps every single day to achieve long-term results.

The Truth Cycle

I can't make you believe anything I've said, but I can show you why you should. And I can show you how you can. You can rewrite the lies into truth and change your life. Forever.

Positive change starts with a single choice.

Change starts with a single choice birthed out of a deep knowing that there has to be more. The choice is fueled by a desire for something better, a desire to get out of the negative loop in which you are stuck, and a want to move towards something different because you know this can't be all life is supposed to be.

The single choice means you take productive action.

You have to do something before you get something. You have to do the work before you get the paycheck. There's nowhere that you get paid first, and then you do the job. You do the job, and then you get paid. You put in the work, and then you lose the weight. You eat right, and you're healthy. It's always the work first and the results second. The choice to change means choosing to do something about your situation and following through until the end.

The productive action creates faith in the expected net result.

The delayed growth of the bamboo tree is like faith. You have to work and believe that what you are doing will pay off, even when you don't see. Faith is confidence in what we hope for and assurance about what we do not see. We understand that the universe was created by God, who spoke it into existence.

HOW TO REWRITE THE LIE

Fueled by a desire to change, a want for something different

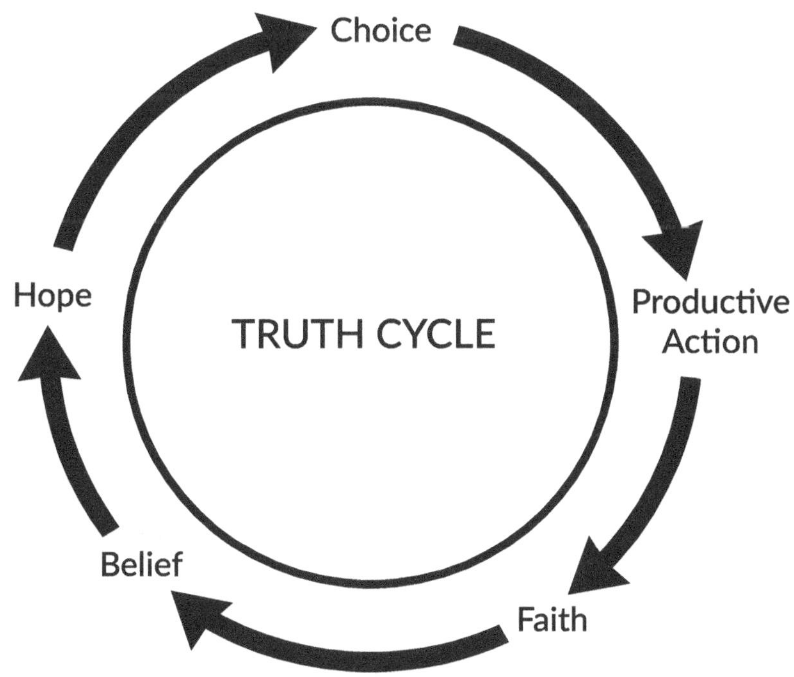

Challenging: Requires effort and consistency

The Furthest Distance Between Two Points

We know that what is seen is not made out of what is visible. The universe was created by the Word of God, but it was already there. God just spoke it into existence. To have faith, you must accept that your future can look different, even if it's not visible to you. This is the challenge. You will not see immediate results. You have faith that things are going to be different in your life. When you start working out on day one, you will not see any results. Everyone knows someone in their life who is buff or in great shape. Everybody knows somebody who has abs of steel. But on day one, nothing happens. On day two, nothing happens. On day seventeen, you finally start to see something. On day thirty-four, you really start to see the changes, much like the bamboo tree after five years. The initial evidence is not visible. As you walk out the action, the result of the work goes from invisible to visible.

In the natural world, when society looks at a kid who grew up with a single mother on food stamps living in HUD apartments, what is seen is, "There's no way that kid ever adds up to anything." Because he's a product of his surroundings, the kid ends up becoming a drug addict and an alcoholic, which is exactly where he was predicted to be. Our environment often dictates our growth. If you put a shark in a small fish tank, it only grows to eight inches. The same species of shark living in the ocean grows to twenty feet. The natural assumption is that I would not amount to anything. The natural sees what I was supposed to be: someone struggling through life, which I became. What faith shows is the reality and evidence of what we cannot see. When we walk out faith, it turns what cannot be seen into what can be seen. Faith and actions work together, and faith is completed by what we do. My life did not come from anything that can be seen.

In faith, I spoke what I wanted to exist. "God, I would like to make a certain dollar amount a year. I don't want to struggle. I want to help other people. I want to speak to people about homelessness and to drug addicts and alcoholics. I want to give people hope. I want to give people an opportunity. I want to change the world. That's written on the wall of my office, "I want to change the world. One interaction at a time." Faith is exactly that—expecting what we cannot see to become a reality. When I spoke all that in faith, I was in jail. When I walked out of jail, I was making $11 an hour but professing that I was a millionaire and a great father, even though I hadn't been in my children's lives for 15 years. My actions created my faith, allowing me to speak out what I could not yet see.

Faith generates the belief that you CAN be what you choose to do.

You can't start with belief. I can't make you believe something, but I can help you make the right choice. That's why change always begins with choice. To change the lies for truth, you must change your beliefs. Once the belief has changed, the choices change. It becomes effortless. This book is about changing what you believe. So, if you're a drug addict and alcoholic, then what you have to believe is that you can be clean and sober. I never believed I could live a happy life without alcohol and drugs. I never believed it was possible. Then I decided I might as well try it. I made the choice, and I took the action. I spoke out that I was no longer a drug addict and an alcoholic, creating the belief that it was true. I believed in what I could not see because God is too good to not believe. I knew that if God made other people sober and clean, he would do it for me.

The Furthest Distance Between Two Points

The belief is what keeps you going because it produces the hope of where you WILL be.

When we lack hope, we can become physically, emotionally, and spiritually sick. We slowly die inside. But a hope fulfilled brings us life. You can believe in hope because hope doesn't fail us. To have hope, you must walk it out even when you don't see it, which is both action and faith. Action, faith, belief, and hope are all connected. The action creates the faith, which produces the belief in the hope.

Gratitude becomes the fuel to make the next positive choice.

As hope builds and change becomes visible, gratitude results, becoming the new fuel for the truth cycle. Gratitude fuels the continuous choice to take the action. The action makes the faith complete. Faith makes you believe. The belief gives you hope. Hope gives you gratitude. Gratitude fuels the next positive choice, and the cycle continues.

Gratitude then becomes a daily choice because the process is a long-term commitment and takes work. Each step of the cycle requires effort. There will be bad days. When I'm having a bad day, I'm able to take all the bad thoughts captive in my mind because I've made a commitment to choose gratitude. But it's not my own strength that changes my heart. It's God's Spirit inside me that gives me the power to demolish all the negative thoughts, reverse them, and believe them.

As you walk out the truth cycle, no matter where you are in the process and regardless of your current circumstances, you must choose to be grateful.

Choosing gratitude brings joy. Joy is what God gives us, along with love, peace, patience, kindness, goodness, gentleness, and self-control. Gratitude doesn't just become the fuel; it encompasses and surrounds the whole circle. The gratitude of where you're at creates the hope for you to continue persevering.

The Lie Cycle

Negative change starts with a single choice.

The truth cycle is where we are supposed to live, but many of us get stuck in a cycle of lies. "I'm not good enough. I'm unworthy enough. Nobody loves me." Satan convinces us the lies are true because he is a liar himself. He is incapable of truth because there is no truth in him. When he speaks lies, he speaks his native language, which is why he is called the father of lies. The lies that we believe become our truth. We come in agreement with Satan and believe what he is telling us. The choice we make is then fed by lies and wrong beliefs. We partner with an enemy who wants to steal our future and kill and destroy us as we give in to our selfish desires.

The single choice is a destructive action.

Fueled by selfishness, the chosen action is destructive instead of productive, shielding us from the pain caused by the lies that we believe. The lie I believed, "I'm not good enough," led to a lot of the bad choices in my destructive behavior, and because I didn't feel the consequences of my actions, I kept doing them. I was de-

sensitized to jail, and I cared nothing about a lasting relationship. I didn't care about anything except getting high, being drunk, and having sex. I had nothing in life, no relationships, no depth, no material possessions. I had a bag of clothes for years and went from one place to another place to another place. I enjoyed it even though I felt empty. The false joy fed the destructive actions. I would go get high, and then, as I was coming down in the middle of it at the bar, I would go get high again.
The destructive action creates despair.

The destructive action leads to more destructive choices, resulting in a feeling of despair. I would wake up next to a girl I didn't know or wake up in some foreign place after an all-night party or not sleep at all, and then I would think, "I've got to quit doing this. This is destroying my life. I can't believe I'm still doing this." I would be flooded with regret. I would get to this point of despair that nothing would ever change.

Despair generates negative beliefs about self. "This is all I'm ever going to be. I'm just a drug addict. I'm just a loser. I'm not good enough." I believed them all. The lies persisted, feeding the behavior. The negative belief produces hopelessness.

Despair creates a negative belief that everything is hopeless. The hopelessness feeds the empty lies. The empty lies convince us that we will never be anything in society and that there's nothing more out there for us. Hopelessness causes us to avoid people and responsibilities and often leads to the lie that life has no meaning. We walk around feeling empty and believing that life is meaningless.

FUELED BY SELFISHNESS

Results in self-gratification which fuels the continous choice to take negative action

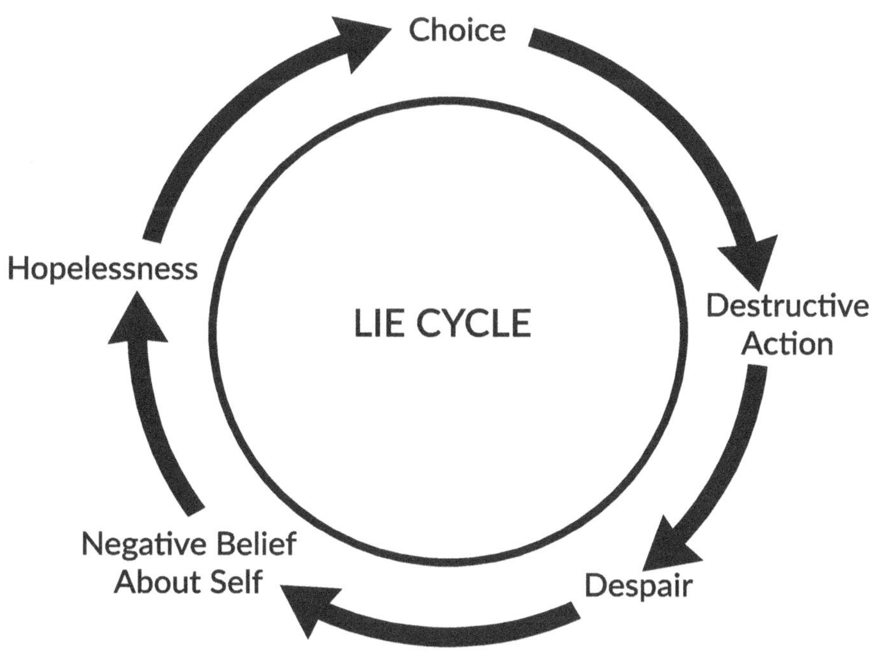

EASY; Immediate Gratification

The Furthest Distance Between Two Points

Self-gratification becomes the new fuel to make the next negative choice.

Self-gratification is when we satisfy our desires. We indulge in what we want. While the truth cycle fuels itself on gratitude towards Jesus, the lie cycle's fuel is gratification towards self. The lies are fueled by self-enjoyment. "That's good for me. When I do this, I'm getting enjoyment. It makes me feel good." I never cared about anyone else. I chose my own selfishness, and I chose me every single time. And it was easier. While the truth cycle is an investment in the future, the lie cycle is getting what we want right now. It's immediate gratification. It doesn't take work. The path of self-gratification and immediate gratification is so much easier than serving others, so much more satisfying than delaying what I want, and so much easier than being responsible.

Satan works to keep the lie going, and I know why. I kept the lies going. I was lying to everybody. When I was manipulating people and in my addiction and getting money from people for sex, drugs or alcohol, or whatever it was, I just told another lie and another lie and another lie. I continued the cycle of lies for self-gratification. The only reason you sin is because you like what's happening. You like the results of the choice. You sin because it feels good. That's what I did. I liked it. It felt good. I chose drugs and alcohol for my gratification. But it was more than that. It was self-exaltation. It's what Satan did. He tried to exalt himself above God. That's why he's not in Heaven anymore. He used to be the most beautiful angel and God's right-hand angel, but he wanted to be God. God removed him and all his followers, and he fell like lightning from heaven. Now, he wages war with God and God's creation. Unfortunately, many of us have fallen into Satan's trap. Today's world has a love for self. We are a selfie society seeking immediate self-gratification. The television tells me I can have sex with whomever I want. My phone gives me access to porn and anything I desire. It doesn't matter that God tells us to be pure, that purity is better, and that it's foundational to a great marriage and an amazing life with Jesus. But this feels good right now, so we make the decision to satisfy ourselves in the moment, and the cycle continues.

Intersecting Truths

When we are stuck in the cycle of lies, we create a series of negative loops based on our destructive choices. The opposite is also true. When we take a bunch of truth cycles and put them together, we create a bunch of positive loops of choice, action, belief, hope, and gratitude. In the middle of all the concentric circles is God's perfect pleasing will for our lives. Where the circles intersect, we find our purpose. Purpose is the combination of our God-given gifts, talents, and abilities to be used for something greater than ourselves.

Your purpose will always reveal itself when you allow your life to reflect Christ. You can then walk out who God created you to be with the gifts, talents, and abilities he gave you. It sounds complex, but it is so easy. It's just walking out what you are already naturally good at, using all that God gave you to benefit everyone else around you. The choice is the opposite of pride. You walk out your purpose when you do the complete opposite of selfishness, which is to serve others above yourself. Your choices are selfless, not selfish.

The Furthest Distance Between Two Points

The continuous truth cycles change our beliefs, which change the lies into truths. Jesus tells us that the truth will set us free. We are no longer stuck in a prison of enemy lies where Satan is the warden. Now, I walk in freedom. I can't comprehend drug use. I hate the idea of me not being faithful to my wife, or doing drugs, or smoking a cigarette. I smoked a cigar on my trip to Mexico. The guy I was with asked if I smoked them. I used to really, really love them, but I've never smoked one sober. So, I said, "You know what, let's get a cigar. Let's smoke a cigar. Let's find out." I took two puffs of it. It was disgusting. I just started laughing. I told him, "It's a God-thing. I just can't, so thanks. Sorry. Didn't mean to waste the money on the cigar." It's funny how all these choices are so easy now that I'm living in this truth cycle. I thought, "God, I'm sorry." Years ago, that never would've even triggered in my brain. Yes, the path that got me here was a long-term commitment, but Jesus walked by my side the entire way. Now, all those things that I had to work on have become effortless. The work was worth it. I am living a life I could never have imagined.

I used to be a gambler. I took risks. If you told me back then, when I was a drug addict, that I would be living this life, I would not have put money on that bet. I not only couldn't see it, but I also couldn't even dream of it. But God knew. He created me for a purpose, and the life I was living wasn't my purpose. The life I live now is what God created me to be. But I had a part in it. I chose to step into the cycle of truth. You also have a choice. You can choose to stay in a cycle of lies or choose to step into a future of truth.

FUELED BY SELFISHNESS

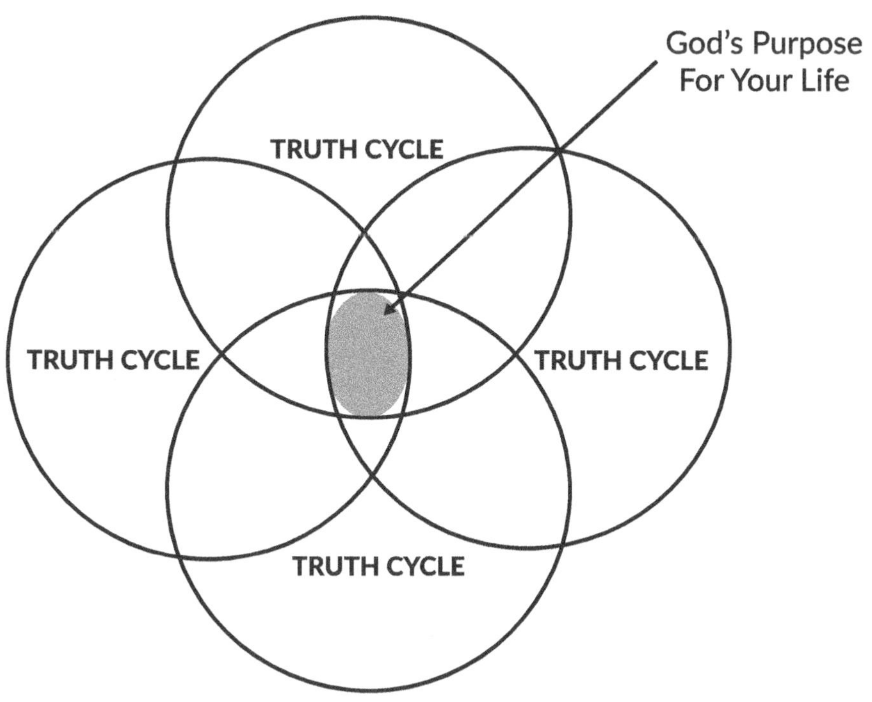

The Furthest Distance Between Two Points

What cycle do you choose?

How to Rewrite the Lie

We can't control the negative thoughts that pop into our heads. Unfortunately, as men, we think things about women all the time. And I think women think things about men, too. They just don't talk about it as often. While you can't control your thoughts, you can control what you do with them. You start by saying something grateful. When I thought, "I don't belong here," I would say, "Lord, thank you for allowing me to be a member of the Patriot Golf Club. Lord, thank you so very much that I get to influence other people's lives." Then I would say the complete opposite of the thought, "I'm the best dude in this room." I made sure that I overwrote and reprogrammed my brain.

You have to rewrite the lie into a truth.

We do that by taking the lie Satan tries to convince us of and find truth from what God's Word tells us.

Lie: I'm fatherless.
Truth: Galatians 3:26. I'm God's child.

Lie: I'm alone.
Truth: John 15:15. I'm Jesus' friend.

Lie: I have nothing to offer.
Truth: Genesis 1:28. I'm fruitful; I'm purposeful.

Lie: I am unworthy and unacceptable.
Truth: Romans 15:7. Christ accepted me.

Lie: I have no confidence.
Truth: Proverbs 28:1. The righteous are as bold as a lion.

Lie: I don't have what I need.
Truth: Philippians 4:19. God supplies all my needs.

Lie: I am addicted.
Truth: John 8:36. Jesus set me free.

Lie: I am the same person I always was.
Truth: 2 Corinthians 5:17. The old has passed away. The new has come.

The action leads to a change in the heart. But you must do the actionable step first. As you follow the truth cycle model, you will find that actionable steps get easier and easier. If you've never tried being sober, try it. See what happens. Decide what you want to change. Then, be sober before you're sober. Choose to be that before you truly are. That's faith. Tell yourself you are sober. Believe that you can and will be sober because you are choosing sobriety. Hold onto the hope that your life is changing and your future will be brighter, and give thanks continually.

Then walk out the truth.

Remove yourself from parties. Walk away from bars. Spend more time with your family. Admit that you made a mistake. Enter a rehabilitation program. Start walking it out today. When someone comes to me and says they want to make money, I tell them to start selling lemonade. Start selling candy. Start repackaging stuff from wholesale businesses. Do whatever they want to do. There are so many ways to make money. I coach businessmen and women. I tell them that if they want to be a business owner or an entrepreneur, they should start reading books by successful people. Start doing something to walk out the truth that you are believing.

How do you do that? Make the next right choice. You know what that is. Everybody knows at any given moment what they're supposed to do. Start reading the Bible. Then, do something physical. Work out at home or in a gym. Then read something to make you better. Then go to your job, whatever that job may be. If you don't have a job, go knock on doors and ask if you can mow yards, wash windows, clean out gutters, rake leaves, or whatever. Go do your job to the absolute best of your ability, whether you are cooking fries at McDonald's, an engineer on the world's biggest bridge, or the CEO of Walmart. Not like a bumper sticker or a t-shirt that says, "I gave it my best," but legitimately, give it your best. Work as if you are working for Jesus. Give him your best. Give others your best. If you see something that needs to be done, do it. Even if it's not your job, just do what needs to be done. Serve people. Go home. Love your family. Love everyone around you. Pray. Read God's Word. Commit to working out, reading a book, growing, and getting better every single day. It's such a simple, simple equation. It's like an equation on a mathematical board in algebra class. Life = X + Y + Z. It really is that simple.

But Satan is going to try to convince you it's not. He'll not only try to attack you, but he'll also complicate your life. I can see now that certain situations and opportunities presented to me in the past were strategically put there by Satan. I chose to work for him. I destroyed myself. I lived a life to give him glory as opposed to building my testimony for the glory of Christ.

If we look at the truth cycle again, the ability to overcome Satan starts with creating a habit of making the right choices. Those choices come from the foundation of who you are in Christ and being able to have and understand that God is your Father and that Jesus is the Victor. Knowing Jesus already won the battle gives us the ability to armor ourselves against the lies of Satan. Then, when the trials come, because they will, and when an attack comes, and things happen to you, you can stand up and fight. Jesus is our model. We find his strategies by reading about his life in the books of Matthew, Mark, Luke, and John. Through the stories of his life and through parables, we see what happens when we make the right choices. The problem is that wrong choices have short-term results. "If I go sell these drugs today, I get this money today," as opposed to, "If I build Living Water, it will take years." You can choose the short-term. You can choose immediate gratification, but you will never change the legacy of your life. You can leave a negative legacy, or you can leave a negative legacy behind you. You don't have to identify as the lie you believe or your past or current surroundings. You don't have to carry that with you. I never had to assimilate to my surroundings. You can change your surroundings by changing who you are. You don't have to be what you were. You are defined by who God says you are.

I was a thief. I AM a business owner and mentor. I was an addict who lived in a dope house. I AM sober, healthy, safe, and contributing to society. I was lost and hopeless. I AM set free and hopeful. I was fatherless. I AM a child of God.

The Furthest Distance Between Two Points

If you are able to take care of yourself, have the ability to articulate thoughts, and can speak, you have everything you need. I can't make you believe it, but I can show you that it's a fact. There are people changing their lives and living out their best every single day. Search the internet for stories about people who are less advantaged than you to show yourself that there are people who choose to be better than their circumstances. Look up "Chris Nikic." He has Down Syndrome. He did an Iron Man. No matter where you're at in life and what's going on in your life, there are always people who have come out of way worse situations than you. You can do it. God has gifted me with certain abilities, talents, and skills. He has chosen to surround me with an unbelievable group of people, some he brought to me and some I consciously sought out to be a part of my life. Go seek out a mentor. Go seek out somebody to challenge you. Go seek out somebody to hold you accountable. Go seek out somebody to call you out on your bad decisions and develop those relationships. Reciprocate and serve those people and watch how quickly you begin to grow. You'll be ninety feet tall. If God did it for me, he will do it for you because there's nothing special about Josh Wilson except that God decided I needed to be born.

The Biggest Lie Told

Johnny McGrew told me nothing in life is free, but respectfully, he was wrong. There's one thing in life that is free. I told you our company name, Living Water Irrigation, is based on John 7:38. The story is about a woman at a well.

At noon, in the hottest part of the day, Jesus goes to a well to get a drink. Shortly after he sits down, a woman comes to get water, too, which is not normal because all the other women of the town fetch water in the morning when it is cool. This particular woman came during the day to avoid all the other women in the town. She is an outcast in society. When Jesus sees the woman, he asks her if she would get him a drink. She responds by asking him why he would ask her to give him a drink since her people, the Samaritans, and his people, the Jews, hated each other. He responds by telling her, "If you knew the gift of God and who it is that asks you for a drink, you would have asked him and he would have given you living water." She asks Jesus where to get the living water so she won't be thirsty and has to keep coming to the well to drink. He then lovingly brings to light her sin that she is living with a man who is not her husband and that she had five husbands before him. At first, she thinks he is a prophet because he knows things about her that he shouldn't. But then, Jesus reveals to her who he is. Not only does he reveal he is the Savior she's been looking for, but he pursues her despite her sin. She believes he is who he says he is and runs home to tell everyone that she met Jesus, the Savior, the living water.

When we get thirsty, we need a drink. But many of us, instead of reaching for fresh, living water that will satisfy and sustain us, reach for dirty lake water. We are always looking for clean water but can't seem to find it because we look in the wrong places. We have to ask ourselves these questions: What am I seeking? What am I chasing? Where am I finding my pleasure? What am I looking for to take away my pain and bring me joy? What fulfills me? What satisfies me?

When we are in the cycle of lies, we seek an answer to those questions in drugs, alcohol, women, pornography, and lying. That's how I answered those questions. I filled the void with dirty water that left me empty, which kept me asking the same questions because I was always thirsty. There was a long period of time in my life when I felt nothing. I shut myself off and was desensitized to the world. I felt nothing, no joy, happiness, anger, or sorrow, because I couldn't find an answer to my questions, so I gave up seeking. There was a hole, an empty space that I couldn't fill. Life was hollow. It was like a missing puzzle piece in my life. Even though drug addicts always have people around them, there are moments when they find themselves alone, and that's when this emptiness and loneliness inside causes us to start searching for something. We seek something to fill it, so we look in the dope houses, the bars, and the beds of multiple people. There is no light. It's dark. But even in the seeking, there's never a search for truth.

Let me give you the truth. Jesus is the truth. When we are out of a relationship with Jesus, something is always missing. What we are seeking is Jesus. My entire life changed when I changed my answer to all the questions I previously asked myself. My answer now is Jesus Christ crucified. There is no other answer. Whether we are angry, happy, joyful, sorrowful, have highs or lows, successes or failures, the answer is always Jesus. He is the only one who will fill the void in our lives. The answer to every question in this life is Jesus. Should I go into this business? Jesus. Should I talk to my wife like this? Jesus. Should I think this thought? Jesus.

So, truly, that statement that nothing is free in life is a lie. Salvation is free, and God's love requires no charge whatsoever. The only requirement is to do what the woman at the well did: believe that Jesus is who he says he is. Jesus is the way, the truth, and the life.

11
THE FINAL DECISION

This book is about choices. You can make positive choices or negative choices. Imagine you are standing in the middle of a crossroads. Behind you are all these roads winding in every direction. In front of you is a single straight and narrow path, and you must choose which way you want to go.

Choice A means sobriety and success. You choose to go forward. Do you want to get well?

Choice B means drugs and destruction. You choose to go backward. Do you want to stay the same?

This single choice to step off the road you are currently on, and step on the road you are supposed to be on is a choice that will change the rest of your life. This is a critical point in your life. This crossroad is where I saw some friends get stuck because of their desire to remain where they were, refusing to overcome their current place in life. They followed a bunch of paths leading nowhere. I knew if I was going to change my course, I had to act. I had to change my mindset and change what I was doing. So, I did. And I never looked back.

How did I do it? How was I able to change the course of my life and choose the straight and narrow path? Jesus. The answer is always Jesus. This book is not just about choices but also about getting well. My journey started with Jesus asking me, "Do you want to get well?" This was my first choice. Like the man lying beside the pool waiting for something to happen and the woman at the well living a life of sin, I had to choose Jesus.

Choice Jesus means leaving behind who you once were and taking hold of who you can become. Choice Jesus means freedom, joy, and living a life you never could have dreamed was possible. Choice Jesus means peace in the presence of chaos.

The greatest choice you will ever make is if you choose to give your life to Jesus today. The question I have for you is, "Do you want to get well?" If your answer is like mine that day in jail, you might be yelling, "YES! YES! I want to get well!" Your first step is to confess with your mouth that Jesus is Lord and believe in your heart that God raised him from the dead by saying the following prayer out loud:

Sinner's Prayer:

Jesus, I acknowledge that I am a sinner in need of a Savior, and I ask for your forgiveness. I believe that you are Jesus Christ, Son of the Living God, who died for my sins and rose from the dead. I turn from my sins and invite you to come into my heart and life. I want to trust and follow you from now on as my Lord and Savior.

12
A HEART OF GRATITUDE

Welcome to the family! You just took the first step to the rest of your life. You guaranteed your eternity with Jesus in heaven, and no matter what happens in the day-to-day pains, struggles, and distresses of this world, you are part of a family of brothers and sisters in Christ who will always be here for you to help you through life. You also just took your first step to being able to walk a life full of gratitude.

Physiologically, you cannot smile and be in a bad mood. That's why I have a book sitting in my office. It's called Dad Jokes by Kathryn and Ross Petras, and they are hilarious. They're all clean. "Why do seagulls fly over the sea? Because if they flew over the bay, they'd be bagels." You can't be in a bad mood and read this book. "Why were people so excited when the shovel was invented? Because it was a groundbreaking invention." You just can't be in a bad mood. If you're laughing, you can't be mad.

I am the opposite of who I was. I slept on so many couches. People I knew would pay for me to stay a week at a hotel or offer me a spare bedroom. Those friends and family helped me stay alive. I probably wouldn't have made it if I had not had a warm place to sleep, shelter, and food. Basic needs weren't a priority to me. When you're an addict, your hierarchy of needs goes out the window. You don't think about food, water, shelter, security, and safety. Those life necessities aren't a priority. All you're thinking about is how can I get high next. What can I do to get the next thing that I want? I wasn't grateful for anyone or anything they did for me. Now, I live a life of gratitude. My fuel is gratitude. Some might joke and say it's Dr. Pepper because I have a Dr. Pepper fountain in my house. I like Dr. Pepper. But my fuel is gratitude. I am fueled by my closeness and constant communion with Jesus.

Amy and I took a vacation to Cabo, San Lucas, Mexico. Early in the morning, when Amy was still sleeping, I decided to watch the sunrise and spend time with God. I got up when it was dark and headed to the beach. As I sat there, I had this overwhelming flood of gratitude. I've struggled for a long time to feel worthy of where I am in life. I can name a hundred guys who are smarter, better looking, better speakers, more educated, more successful, and are stuck in bad jobs, making $15 an hour, or are addicted to drugs and alcohol. I've struggled with the thoughts, "Why me, God? Why do I get to live this life?"

I sat on the beach crying, thinking about my life, where I was then versus where I am now, and reflecting on the life God gifted me. It's just remarkable. I can't find an adjective. I can't come up with the words, and I know I won't be able to find one because I've searched. I can't find a word to describe the depth of my gratitude. How do you thank God for all he's done? Thank you just isn't enough. I fully recognize the unbelievable favor and a hundred-fold return on my effort. That's why I'm so driven by gratitude. There's a song called "Too Good To Not Believe" by Brandon Lake and Cody Carnes. Throughout the song, they repeat the line, "Don't tell me he can't do it." It's true. Don't tell me he can't do it because I am a testimony that he can, and he will.

I have a passion for making sure that everyone understands what God has done and brought me through. It's the Matthew West song, "My Story, Your Glory." I sat there that morning on the beach, watching the sun come up and listening to the waves crashing on the shore. It was so beautiful and so peaceful. No one else was there except God and me, and I kept thinking, "This is my life." But it's not just my life. It happens every day to others, too, and it can happen to you.

Here's what I know is on the other side of the labor, trenches, and pain—freedom and peace. There is a peace that comes when you walk with God and walk out what He's designed for your life. We all have a purpose in this life that God placed in us before we were conceived. He formed us in our mother's wombs, knew us before we were born, and set us apart as his children. I've talked to a lot of pastors and people who serve, some of them in unpaid positions, and I see the same thing in every single one of them when they talk about their calling and where God has them. They are full of joy.

I want so desperately for people to live my life. I live an amazing life. But it's not about the watch I wear, the truck I drive, the money I make, or the fact that I play golf at a country club. It's about me being able to make an impact for God here on earth before I get to be with him in eternity. It's not a matter of how much you have. It's a matter of what you do with what you have and how grateful you are for it.

Gratitude should be the fuel for everyone's life. But gratitude is a choice. Grateful people are optimistic. Optimistic people succeed four to five times more than pessimistic people. Optimistic people live longer than pessimistic people. Optimistic people are healthier than pessimistic people. I could keep going. Gratitude is a choice. You must choose to be grateful. We must live a life of gratitude no matter what we have, whether we have a lot or a little, a package of ramen noodles or a steak dinner.

Whenever I'm aggravated, I'll say three things out loud that I'm grateful for to reframe my thinking. I'm coaching four people right now, and every evening before they go to bed, they text me three things they are grateful for and the one win they had during their day. All four of them do not recognize what is all around them. I'm conditioning gratitude. You must choose to find something you are thankful for, even if it's something simple, like breathing. If you woke up today, you have something to be grateful for because there's a whole bunch of people who didn't wake up this morning. Whenever I start to think negative things about my life, like, "I don't belong in this room with super great fathers or super great men or super successful businessmen," I say three things I'm grateful for, including one that I can say every day of my life: I'm grateful my mom saw me sober before she went to be with Jesus.

My Why

None of my life makes sense. That's why I'm so grateful, and that's why I want to articulate what God has done for me over the past ten years. Out of a heart of gratitude, I want to make sure I tell my story for God's glory.

Our vision statement at Living Water is to change the world one interaction at a time.

That's also my personal why: to change the world one interaction, one moment, one person at a time by bringing joy, positivity, and encouragement to others. So now, my focus is pouring into other people and building relationships. Jesus has brought me joy, love, restoration, and reconciliation. I am so passionate about God and what He has done for me. I want to share my story because I know God will do that for every single one of us. When we cry out to Jesus, He hears us and answers.

My purpose is to inspire, motivate, and provide hope. God set me up to be able to relate to all different groups of people. I thought my purpose was to make money and give it away. While that is a big function of my life, had I not been through all that I have, I couldn't help certain people. I can talk to drug addicts. I can talk to athletes. I can talk to Mexicans and Caucasians. I can talk to billionaires. God showed me I could communicate with anyone He put in front of me after I was invited on a chartered yacht in Los Cabos by a man who owns a billion dollar business. The last time I was in a room with a bunch of billionaire guys sitting next to me at the Patriot Country Club, all I could think was, "I'm just a ditch digger. I'm just a dude installing greens. I shouldn't be here." Now, I can talk to someone with more money than I will ever see, and I belong there. But I also belong at the HUD Apartments in North Tulsa, talking with the dope dealer who statistically won't make it out of there. Both people receive the same message. Jesus is the better way.

God is a God of grace and of love. He helped me through Celebrate Recovery and the Step Study Program to get healed and whole from my issues with unworthiness, insecurity, broken relationships, and abandonment. God knows what we need when we don't even know what we need. My grandfather died when I was in jail. For years, I was torn up about the fact that I missed his funeral. But God knew what was best. I realized years later that had I been free when my grandfather died, I wouldn't have been sober to work through his death.

That's God's Grace

There's no greater high than to help transform someone's life because you're willing to spend thirty minutes a week with them. It's altruistic, but I'm not sure who gets more out of it. Maximus has done way more for me than I've ever done for him. My hope is that I'm able to impress upon Maximus some amazing things and, pour into his life and be faithful and consistent in all the things I haven't been with my kids. I get so much more out of that relationship than he does from me.

I've been coaching a young man I met through recovery. He's trying to start a business, and I've been helping him. One day, he called me and asked if I would be a groomsman in his wedding. I was so shocked. He said, "I can't think of a better person to stand up there." To see a person's transformation is so rewarding. It's way better than any high, any run at a casino, and any woman except Amy. When you take kids who the world says aren't supposed to be anything but exactly what they currently are and exactly what their parents are, and they rise above their circumstances, their reach is exponential. Satan will attempt to stop what God is trying to do. His goal is to prevent kids from finding their purpose so he can destroy their story. That's what he tried to do to me, and that's what he tries to do to us all.

Hope Is Alive is a faith-based, non-profit organization that works to radically change the lives of addicts and those who love them. Part of their ministry provides houses for a sober living community. Amy and I met them three years ago. When Living Water started to take off, we, as a Living Water team, committed to buying houses for people who graduated out of recovery. The program is tough. They make you process why you used drugs, why you did alcohol, why you were addicted to pornography or sex, or whatever your addiction is. I had the privilege of watching ten people graduate. I was fired up for days because I recognized that my obedience, faithfulness, and hard work provided opportunities for addicts the same way that other people provided opportunities for me. I never would have found recovery had people not sacrificed their time, effort, and energy and not been so willing to sit with me when I needed help. All I can think now is I have to do more. There've been four people that I know over the last four months who have died of an overdose. I have to do more.

That is what's next for me. To do more. I want to tell my story, and I hope and pray that people will hear the message and understand that when we choose Jesus, He can do anything. When we choose to be obedient, trust God, and go fervently after Him, in the same way we've previously chosen to go in the direction of destruction, God can do anything. God is a God of greatness. God is a God of excellence. He wants excellence for all of us. Through my story, I hope you'll recognize that if you remove the limits in your life, God can do absolutely anything and that your future can be all you choose for it to be.

The title of this book is The Furthest Distance Between Two Points: From Drugs and Destruction to Sobriety and Success. But success

The Furthest Distance Between Two Points

doesn't have anything to do with money. Don't get me wrong; having some financial freedom and security is a great place to be. I previously defined success as overcoming. While I believe that's still a working definition, the real definition of success is having a strong, powerful relationship with God and being in constant communion with Jesus. What does that look like?

Success is going out and sharing God's story about Jesus and your story about what God did in your life.

Success is deep relationships with other believers.

Success is positively impacting the world.

Success is being a great father.

Success is generationally helping to change the legacy that is set forth.

Success is you reaching the potential that you have.

Success is impacting the world the way that only YOU can.

Success is waking up each morning with gratitude for what you have.

Success is a choice.

13
NOW WHAT

When I gave my life to Jesus and chose to become a better person, I used resources to help me. Celebrate Recovery was a large portion of my healing process. The following is the website to find a local meeting.

www.celebraterecovery.com

There are other steps I took to make sure I succeeded. To stay on the right road, you must remove all the negative people in your life. Don't talk to anyone who's not providing positivity into your world. Don't talk to anyone that you ever got drunk with, anyone you've ever done drugs with, or any woman with whom you had sex. Delete them all and find a new community. Before my sobriety, there were only two people with whom I still communicated with, and neither of them had ever had a drinking or drug problem. Other than those two friends, I have zero relationships from my past. I don't talk to any of those people. I don't associate with them.

I think it's important that you check the facts of my story so that you have no doubt that what I'm telling you is true. My address growing up was 4920 South Mingo. You can google it. It's Mingo Manor Apartments in Tulsa, Oklahoma. I have it memorized from when I was a little kid. It looks a whole lot better now. There's a lot of things built around it. My phone number was 918-622-8719. You can find all my arrests, too. Look up Pawnee City, Muskogee County, Tulsa County, Rogers County, and Stephens County, Oklahoma. If you look up Muskogee, Oklahoma, you'll find my home repair fraud felony, which makes no sense from the world's perspective because now, I own multiple businesses that work on homes. Don't feel like you shouldn't be where you're at because our God is a God of grace. God's grace is what has allowed me to be here. You don't have to believe what I'm telling you. I understand that faith is very hard. Trust is also very hard. Just go check the facts.

But those facts do not define me anymore. And the facts of your life won't define you anymore. You're no longer who you were or what you used to do. You are what you choose to do now. If you choose the right path and do what you're supposed to do, then you can go where God wants you to and step into the mission, purpose, and calling that God has for your life. Once you do that, you can pour out the love of Jesus on others. You will be able to go out and share the gifts that God gave you with the world. You'll be able to go out and impact people in a truly life-changing way. You can make an eternal impact on God on earth and help people see what they can do and what they can be if they choose to.

Your future is so beautiful. Your future is so bright. I've got to wear shades!

I'm so thankful that you have chosen to join this journey with me, and I'm so grateful that you've chosen to read this book. Please go forward from here, knowing that God has a great plan for your life. Understand that if you remove the limits, if you absolutely go forward fervently with confidence, consistency, and discipline, there is absolutely nothing God can't do. Know that God is with you and is for you and will never leave you.

I hope this book serves as a message of hope and will help influence those who have lived the life I lived or are currently living like that. My hope and prayer are that you will believe that something better is on the other side and decide to take action.

My story is living proof that life is better when you are sober.

If you read this book and you are really struggling with your journey, whether it is drugs, alcohol, business, or something else, I want you to reach out to me. I was put on this earth to help people, so if you need help, reach out to me at Josh@transformed.consulting, and I would be honored to help in any way I can.

If you read this book and have OVERCOME something huge, you are a story of success, redemption, and transformation. I would love to hear from you as well. Please send me your story so we can share and encourage each other!

Gracias,

Josh Wilson

ACKNOWLEDGEMENTS

To **God:** Thank you for your grace, unmerited favor, and all the skills, talents, and abilities you have gifted me with.

To **Grandpa:** For teaching me what it looks like to serve others first. For your work ethic and honoring your word. You are the smartest man I have ever known.

To **Amy:** There never should have been a second date. Thank you for being my last first kiss, my helper, my rock, and what drives me to want to come home everyday.

To **Mom:** For pushing me, for challenging me, for always cheering for me and for teaching me what hard work looks like.

To **Jay:** Thank you for taking the job of being the father in my life every day growing up. You were just a kid yourself. Thank you for the competition, for defending my big mouth, and for loving me.

To **Jonas:** Thank you for your heart, your compassion, your empathy, your sympathy, and for teaching me how to care more deeply and to love deeper.

To **My Kids:** For the future and hope!

To **Spencer and Cayenne, Jacob, and Katarina:** Thank you for allowing me the space to be in your lives. And thanks for the amazing grandkids.

To **Maximus DeVore:** For making me more selfless. For teaching me the real importance of commitment and dedication to someone.

To **Robert Meade:** For making me believe that all of this is possible. You are the epitome of inspiration. You taught me: "If I can, you can too!"

To **Bryan Edelman:** For being the most Christ-like example of a man I've ever seen and willingly owning and admitting your flaws!

To **Chris Claybon:** For questioning everything and for always forcing me to look at things in different and better ways.

To **Sean Highberger:** For challenging me to be a better leader and for forcing me to be a better communicator.

To **Nathan Faught:** For matching my energy. For planting seeds with your time, effort, and knowledge.

To **Jonathan Kelly:** My Brother. Our partnership goes so much deeper than business. Thank you for allowing me to chase this new road and for taking care of business. I'm not crying, you are….

To **Kim DeVore:** For this labor of love. For putting all my incoherent words together in such a beautiful way. This book literally would not have been possible without your sacrifice, commitment, and decision to persevere.

To **Jensynn Watts:** For doing all my work. You are so much more than an assistant. You're the worst.

To **Dr. Z:** For all the time and wisdom.

To **Eric Williams:** For teaching me servant leadership.

To **Greg Schuh:** For finance, business, and genius.

To **Lance Lang:** For starting HIA and allowing us to be a part of it. Thank you for the vision and the inspiration to serve others.

To **Addicts:** For the inspiration to stay sober and keep pressing in and on!

To **Entrepreneurs:** For the push.

To **Gary V:** For empathy.

To **Jocko:** For discipline.

To **Andy Frisella:** For no excuses.

To **Simon Sinek:** For defining real leadership.

To **John Maxwell:** For all the leadership books and knowledge.

To **Craig Groeschel:** For actionable, real, leadership techniques.

To **Andy Elliot:** For sales.

To **Vinh Giang:** For communication.

To **Jim Rohn:** For challenges.

To **David Goggins:** For staying hard.

To all the other people who over the years have spent their time, money, energy, and efforts to help me become who I am today and afforded me the opportunity to write this book, thank you. Even though I may not have called you out by name, you are just as equally important in my life. I could go on and on to dozens and hundreds of people who have sacrificed so much to get me to where I am today. I wouldn't be here without all of you.

Disclaimer:

There are several sentences, quotes, and statements that I am 100% positive aren't 100% my words. I just can't remember where I heard them. Please take it as a compliment. I know they impacted my life, and my hope is that they will impact others too.